Student's Book
Stage 4

English in a quarter of the time!

The Callan ® Method was first developed and published
in 1960 by R.K. T. Callan.

Copyright © Callan Works Limited 2014

First edition by R. K. T. Callan, published for the international market in 2012
This second edition by R. K. T. Callan, published for the international market in 2013

Student's Book – Stage 4
978-1-78229-239-5

CALLAN and the CALLAN logo are registered trade marks of
Callan Works Limited, used under licence by Callan Method Organisation Limited

Printed in the EU

Published by

CALLAN METHOD ORGANISATION LTD.
Ivy Dene, 43 Mill Way, Grantchester, Cambridge, CB3 9ND, UK

www.callan.co.uk

- Para obtener la traducción de este prefacio en español, visitar
  www.callan.co.uk/preface/es

- Per una traduzione di questa prefazione in Italiano, visitare il sito
  www.callan.co.uk/preface/it

- Para obter uma tradução deste prefácio em português, visite
  www.callan.co.uk/preface/pt

- Z polskim tłumaczeniem tego wstępu można zapoznać się na stronie
  www.callan.co.uk/preface/pl

- Pour obtenir la traduction de cette préface en français, rendez-vous sur le site
  www.callan.co.uk/preface/fr

- Bu önsözün Türkçe çevirisi için aşağıdaki web adresini ziyaret edin
  www.callan.co.uk/preface/tr

- 本序言的中文翻译，请访问
  www.callan.co.uk/preface/ch

- 前書きの日本語版の翻訳は次ページをご覧ください
  www.callan.co.uk/preface/jp

- للاطلاع على ترجمة هذه المقدمة باللغة العربية يرجى زيارة
  www.callan.co.uk/preface/ar

Welcome to the Callan Method

Learning English with the Callan™ Method is fast and effective!

The Callan Method is a teaching method created specifically to improve your English in an intensive atmosphere. The teacher is constantly asking questions, so you are hearing and using the language as much as possible. When you speak in the lesson, the teacher corrects your grammar and pronunciation mistakes, and you learn a lot from this correction.

The Callan Method teaches English vocabulary and grammar in a carefully programmed way, with systematic revision and reinforcement. In the lesson, there is a lot of speaking and listening practice, but there is also reading and writing so that you revise and consolidate what you have learned.

With the Callan Method, the teacher speaks quickly so that you learn to understand English when it is spoken at natural speed. This also means that everyone is concentrating hard all the time.

English in a quarter of the time

The Callan Method can teach English in a quarter of the time taken by any other method on the market. Instead of the usual 350 hours necessary to get the average student to the level of the Cambridge Preliminary English Test (PET), the Callan Method can take as little as 80 hours, and only 160 hours for the Cambridge First Certificate in English (FCE).

The method is suitable for students of all nationalities, and ages. It requires no equipment (not even a whiteboard) or other books, and can be used for classes at private schools, state schools and universities. It is also possible for students to use the books to practise with each other when they are not at school.

In addition to this, students can practise their English online using the interactive exercises, which are available to students who study at licensed schools. Ask your school for details.

The Callan Method in practice

A Callan Method English lesson is probably very different from lessons you have done in the past. You do not sit in silence, doing a reading comprehension test or a grammar exercise from a book. You do not have 'free conversation', where you only use the English you already feel comfortable with. Of course, activities like this can help you, but you can do them at home with a book, or in a coffee bar. In a Callan Method lesson, you are busy with important activities that you cannot do outside the classroom. You are listening to English all the time. You are speaking English a lot, and all your mistakes are corrected. You learn quickly because you are always surrounded by English. There is no silence and no time to get bored or lose your concentration. And it is also fun!

So, what exactly happens in a Callan Method lesson, and how does it work?

The teacher asks you questions

The Callan Method books are full of questions. Each question practises a word, an expression, or a piece of grammar. The teacher is standing, and asks the questions to the students one by one. You never know when the teacher will ask you, so you are always concentrating. When one student finishes answering one question, the teacher immediately starts to ask the next question.

The teacher speaks quickly

The teacher in a Callan Method lesson speaks quickly. This is because, in the real world, it is natural to speak quickly. If you want to understand normal English, you must practise listening to quick natural speech and become able to understand English without first translating into your language. This idea of not translating is at the centre of the Callan Method; this method helps you to start thinking in English.

Also, we do not want you to stop and think a lot about the grammar while you are speaking. We want you to speak as a reflex, instinctively. And do not worry about mistakes. You will, naturally, make a lot of mistakes in the lessons, but Callan Method teachers correct your mistakes, and you learn from the corrections. When you go home, of course it will help if you read your book, think about the grammar, study the vocabulary, and do all the things that language students do at home – but the lessons are times to practise your listening and speaking, with your books closed!

The teacher says every question twice, and helps you with the answer

In the lesson, the teacher speaks quickly, so we say the questions twice. This way, you have another chance to listen if you did not understand everything the first time.

The teacher then immediately says the beginning of the answer. This is to help you (and 'push' you) to start speaking immediately. So, for example:

Teacher: *"Are there two chairs in this room? Are there two chairs in this room? No, there aren't ..."*

Student (immediately): *"No, there aren't two chairs in this room; there are twelve chairs in this room."*

If the teacher does not 'push' you by giving you the beginning of the answer, you might start to think too much, and translate into your language.

The teacher will speak along with you all the time while you are saying your answer. So, if you forget a word or you are not sure what to say, you will always hear the next word or two from the teacher. You should repeat after the teacher, but immediately try again to continue with the answer yourself. You must always try to continue speaking, and only copy the teacher when you cannot continue alone. That way, you will become more confident and learn more quickly. Never simply wait for help from the teacher and then copy – you will not improve so quickly.

Long answers, with the same grammar as the question

We want you to practise your speaking as much as possible, so you always make complete sentences when you speak in the lesson, using the same grammatical structure as in the question. For example:

Teacher: *"About how many pages are there in this book?"*

Student: *"There are about two hundred pages in that book."*

In this way, you are not just answering a question; you are making full sentences with the vocabulary and the grammar that you need to learn.

Correction by imitation

With the Callan Method, the teacher corrects all your mistakes the moment you make them. The teacher corrects you by imitating (copying) your mistake and then saying the correct pronunciation/form of the word. For example, if you say "He come from Spain", the teacher quickly says "not come - **comes**". This correction by imitation helps you to hear the difference between your mistake and the proper English form. You should immediately repeat the correct word and continue with your sentence. You learn a lot from this correction of your mistakes, and constant correction results in fast progress.

Contracted forms

In the lesson, the teacher uses contractions (e.g. the teacher says "I don't" instead of "I do not"). This is because it is natural to use contractions in spoken English and you must learn to understand them. Also, if you want to sound natural when you speak, you must learn to use contractions.

Lesson structure

Every school is different, but a typical 50-minute Callan lesson will contain about 35 minutes of speaking, a 10-minute period for reading, and a 5-minute dictation. The reading practice and the dictation are often in the middle of the lesson.

In the reading part, you read and speak while the teacher helps you and corrects your mistakes. In the dictation, you practise your writing, but you are also listening to the teacher. So, a 50-minute Callan lesson is 50 minutes of spoken English with no silence!

No chatting

Although the Callan Method emphasises the importance of speaking practice, this does not mean chatting (free conversation). You learn English quickly with the Callan Method partly because the lessons are organised, efficient, fast and busy. There is no time wasted on chatting; this can be done before or after the lesson.

Chatting is not a good way to spend your time in an English lesson. First, only some of the students speak. Second, in a chat, people only use the English that they already know. Third, it is difficult for a teacher to correct mistakes during a conversation.

The Callan Method has none of these problems. All through the lesson, every student is listening and speaking, practising different vocabulary and structures, and learning from the correction of their mistakes. And nobody has time to get bored!

Repeat, repeat, repeat!

Systematic revision

In your native language, you sometimes read or hear a word that you do not already know. You usually need to read or hear this new word only once or twice in order to remember it and then use it yourself. However, when you are learning a foreign language, things are very different. You need to hear, see and use words and grammatical structures many times before you really know them properly. So your studies must involve a system of revision (repeating what you have studied before). This is absolutely essential. If there is no system of revision in your studies, you will forget what you have studied and will not be able to speak or understand better than before.

In every Callan Method lesson, of course you learn new English, practise it, and progress through your book. However, you also do a lot of revision so that you can really learn what you have studied. Your teacher can decide how much revision your class needs, but it will always be an important part of your studies.

Also, because there is a lot of revision, it is not important for you to understand everything the first time; it gets easier. The revision with Callan is automatic and systematic. Every day you do a lot of revision and then learn some new English.

Revision in reading and dictation too

The reading and dictation practice in the lessons is part of Callan's systematic revision as well. First, you learn a new word in the speaking part of the lesson; a few lessons later, you meet it again when you are reading; finally, the word appears in a dictation. This is all written into the Callan Method; it happens automatically.

Correcting your dictations

With the Callan Method, there is little or no homework to do, but it is very important that you correct your dictations. These are printed in your book and so you can easily correct them at home, on the bus, or wherever. It is important to do this because it helps you to learn the written forms of the words you have already studied in earlier lessons.

Your first lessons with the Callan Method

During your first lesson with the Callan Method, all of the questions and some of the vocabulary are new for you; you have not done any revision yet. For this reason, the teacher may not ask you many questions. You can sit and listen, and become more familiar with the method - the speed, the questions, the correction etc.

History of the Callan Method – Robin Callan

 Robin Callan, who passed away in April 2014, was the creator of the Callan Method. In addition to owning the Callan School in London's Oxford Street, he also ran Callan Method Organisation Ltd. This company, now managed by a dedicated team of Callan Method professionals, continues to grow, supplying Callan Method books to schools all over the world.

Robin Callan grew up in Ely, Cambridgeshire, England. In his early twenties, he went to Italy to teach English in Salerno. Although he enjoyed teaching, Robin thought that the way in which teachers were expected to teach their lessons was inefficient and boring. He became very interested in the mechanisms of language learning, and was sure that he could radically improve the way English was taught.

He remained in Italy and started to write his own books for teaching English. He used these in his own classes and, over the following ten years, gained an immense amount of practical experience and a reputation for teaching English quickly and effectively.

When he returned to England, he opened his school in Oxford Street. As the Method became more and more popular with students, the school grew and moved to larger premises. Robin continued to write his Callan Method books, and today the Method is used by schools all over the world.

Robin Callan was always passionate about English literature, especially poetry. For this reason, he bought The Orchard Tea Garden in Grantchester, near Cambridge, which attracts thousands of tourists each year. Throughout the 20th century, it was a popular meeting place for many famous Cambridge University students and important figures from English literature, such as Rupert Brooke, Virginia Woolf and E.M. Forster. Today, it is also home to the Rupert Brooke Museum.

Mr Callan lived in Grantchester for many years, and played an active role in the management of his companies well into his retirement and old age. He left an amazing legacy on which we all continue to build.

How Callan Method Stages compare to CEFR* levels and University of Cambridge General English exams

Common European Framework of Reference

It is difficult to compare the Callan Method books directly with the CEFR levels and Cambridge exams, but below is an approximate guide.

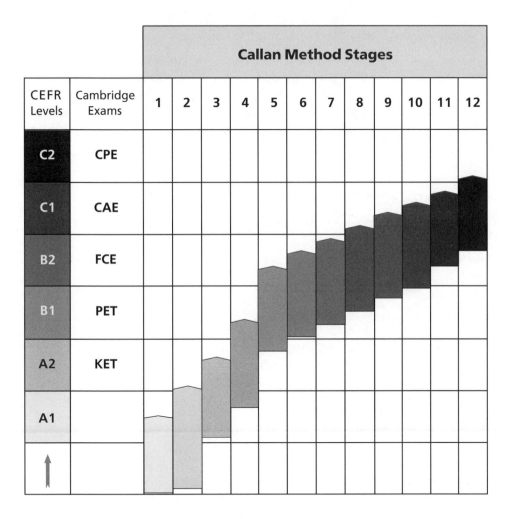

CEFR Levels	Cambridge Exams	Callan Method Stages											
		1	2	3	4	5	6	7	8	9	10	11	12
C2	CPE												
C1	CAE												
B2	FCE												
B1	PET												
A2	KET												
A1													

www.callan.co.uk

STAGE 4

wife – wives **help**

What's the plural of "wife"? The plural of "wife" is "wives"

Do husbands in this country generally help their wives in the house?
Yes, husbands in this country generally help their wives in the house ~ No, husbands in this country don't generally help their wives in the house

If you can't answer a question during the lesson, who helps you to answer it?
If I can't answer a question during the lesson, the teacher helps me to answer it

If you help me, do you think we can lift this table together?
Yes, if I help you, I think we can lift this table together ~ No, if I help you, I don't think we can lift this table together

common

Which is the most common drink in this country besides water?
... is the most common drink in this country besides water

fire

Do you have a fire at home in winter?
Yes, I have a fire at home in winter ~ No, I don't have a fire at home in winter

broad

Which is the broadest street in your town?
... is the broadest street in my town

rich

Who is the richest person you know?   ... is the richest person I know

poor

Name me one of the poorest countries in the world?   ... is one of the
poorest countries in the world

story   bedtime

Do you like reading war stories?   Yes, I like reading war stories
~ No, I don't like reading war stories

Do parents in your country read bedtime stories to their children?
Yes, parents in my country read bedtime
stories to their children ~ No, parents in my
country don't read bedtime stories to their children

express   thought

Can you express a very simple idea quite well in English?   Yes, I can
express a very simple idea quite well in English

Do you think it's easier to express your thoughts in writing or in
speaking?   I think it's easier to express my thoughts in ...

213 ## Irregular verbs   so   change

**The past tenses of some verbs are irregular, and so we do not add "ed" to
form the past tense. Instead, we change the word. For example, the past
of "speak" is "spoke"; the past of "come" is "came" etc.**

What's the past of "speak"?   The past of speak is "spoke"

speak	–	spoke	drive	–	drove
come	–	came	forget	–	forgot
break	–	broke	see	–	saw
wear	–	wore	sit	–	sat
write	–	wrote	eat	–	ate
get up	–	got up	give	–	gave
stand	–	stood	begin	–	began
shine	–	shone	drink	–	drank
take	–	took	sleep	–	slept
tell	–	told			

Which language did we speak during the last lesson? We spoke English during the last lesson

What's the past of "come"? The past of "come" is "came"

What time did you come here last lesson? I came here at ... last lesson

What's the past of "break"? The past of "break" is "broke"

Did you ever break an arm or a leg when you were a little child?
Yes, I broke an arm/a leg when I was a little child ~ No, I never broke an arm or a leg when I was a little child

What did you wear yesterday? I wore ... yesterday

Did I write anything on this piece of paper (or card) last lesson?
Yes, you wrote something on that piece of paper (or card) last lesson ~ No, you didn't write anything on that piece of paper (or card) last lesson

What time did you get up this morning? I got up at ... this morning

Did we stand up after the last lesson? Yes, we stood up after the last lesson

Did the sun shine last week? Yes, the sun shone last week ~ No, the sun didn't shine last week

Did you take any photographs on your last holiday? Yes, I took some photographs on my last holiday ~ No, I didn't take any photographs on my last holiday

Did you tell me your name? Yes, I told you my name

Did anybody in your family drive a car last year? Yes, somebody in my family drove a car last year ~ No, nobody in my family drove a car last year

Did you remember all the new words last lesson from the lesson before that? No, I didn't remember all the new words last lesson from the lesson before that; some I remembered and some I forgot

215 What did you see in this classroom last lesson? I saw some books, some chairs, a teacher etc. in this classroom last lesson

Where did you sit during the last lesson? I sat ... during the last lesson

What did you eat for your lunch yesterday? I ate some ... for my lunch yesterday

Did I give you a dictation last month? Yes, you gave us a dictation last month

When did last season begin? Last season began on ...

What did you drink with your breakfast this morning? I drank some ... with my breakfast this morning

How long did you sleep last night? I slept ... last night

LESSON 42

hill   **around**

Are there any hills around this town/city?

> Yes, there are some hills around this town/city ~ No, there aren't any hills around this town/city

laugh   ·   **comedy**

Do people generally laugh when they're happy or unhappy?

> People generally laugh when they're happy

Do you laugh when you watch comedies?

> Yes, I laugh when I watch comedies

enemy   **Britain**

What's the opposite of the word "friend"?

> The opposite of the word "friend" is enemy

Were Britain and America enemies during the Second World War?

> No, Britain and America weren't enemies during the Second World War; they were friends

castle

Are there any old castles in this town/city?

> Yes, there are some old castles in this town/city ~ No, there aren't any old castles in this town/city

hungry   **noise**

Are you hungry at the moment?

> Yes, I'm hungry at the moment ~ No, I'm not hungry at the moment

Are there a lot of hungry people in some parts of the world today?

> Yes, there are a lot of hungry people in some parts of the world today

Does your stomach make noises when you're hungry? Yes, my
stomach makes noises when I'm hungry

fact **historical** **mathematical**

geographical

Tell me a geographical fact. Mt Everest is the highest
mountain in the world

Tell me a historical fact. The Second World War began in 1939

Tell me a mathematical fact. $\cdot$ $2 + 2 = 4$

Get

We use the word "get" a lot in English, and it has different meanings:

become

The word "get" means "become" when it has an adjective after it. For example, "I am getting hungry" means "I am becoming hungry".

When you get hungry, what do you do? When I get hungry, I eat

Do you think your English is getting better? Yes, I think my
English is getting better

obtain **fetch** **doctor**

When we put a noun after "get", it can mean "receive", "obtain" or "fetch".

About how much does a doctor get *(receive)* a month? A doctor gets
about ... pounds (dollars etc.) a month

Do you get *(receive)* any cards from your friends on your birthday?
Yes, I get some cards from my
friends on my birthday ~ No, I don't
get any cards from my friends on my birthday

Can I get *(obtain)* clothes from a bookshop?

> No, you can't get clothes from a bookshop

Which animal do we get *(obtain)* milk from?

> We get milk from a cow

Will you go and get *(fetch)* a pen for me from the next room, please?

> Yes, I'll go and get a pen for you from the next room

When children are young, do their parents get *(fetch)* them from school each day?

> Yes, when children are young, their parents get them from school each day

Will you get *(fetch)* that book from the table and give it to me, please?

> Yes, I'll get that book from the table and give it to you

get to	reach

If we "get to" a place, it means we arrive (or reach) there.

What time do you generally get to *(arrive at)* school for your lesson?

> I generally get to school at ... for my lesson

219 **Before the words "home", "here" and "there", we do not use the word "to". For example, "I get here at 11 a.m. for my lesson and go home again at 1 p.m.".**

What time do you generally get *(arrive)* home at the end of the day?

> I generally get home at about ... at the end of the day

The verb "get" has other meanings besides the ones here, but its general meanings are "become" (before an adjective) and "obtain" (before a noun). If you are not sure when to use "get", it is better to use the other verb with the same meaning. For example, instead of saying "I get many emails" you can say "I receive many emails".

What are the general meanings of the verb "get"?

> The general meanings of the verb "get" are "become" and "obtain"

If you are not sure when to use "get", what is it better to do?

> If I'm not sure when to use "get", it's better to use the other verb with the same meaning

there was	there were
Is there a picture on that wall?	Yes, there's a picture on that wall
Was there a picture on that wall three lessons ago?	Yes, there was a picture on that wall three lessons ago
Were there any books on the table last lesson?	Yes, there were some books on the table last lesson
Was there a chair in that corner during the last lesson?	No, there wasn't a chair in that corner during the last lesson
Were there any chairs on the table last lesson?	No, there weren't any chairs on the table last lesson

220

die	president
What's the opposite of the verb "to live"?	The opposite of the verb "to live" is "to die"
Do most people die before they're a hundred years old?	Yes, most people die before they're a hundred years old
When did President Kennedy die?	President Kennedy died in 1963

 *Dictation 22*

Mount Everest/ is the highest mountain/ in the world./ The Nile is the longest river/ in the world./ This piece of plastic/ is larger than that one./ Her uncle is/ a very handsome man./ War between two nations/ is unpleasant./ A hundred pence/ make a pound./ I can't measure the increase/ in the quantity of gas/ we're using./ A lemon is a yellow fruit./ Start at the bottom of the road/ and go almost to the top./ The table's heavy./ The date today/ is the twenty-first of October/ 2011.

 *Do Revision Exercise 14*

221	**strong**	**weak**	**physical**

Is whisky a weak drink?

No, whisky isn't a weak drink; it's a strong drink

Are young boys generally physically stronger than men?

No, young boys aren't generally physically stronger than men; they're generally physically weaker than men

Do you speak English with a strong ... accent?

No, I don't speak English with a strong ... accent; I speak it with a strong ... accent

soldier	**army**	**make money**

uniform

Does a soldier make a lot of money these days?

Yes a soldier makes a lot of money these days ~ No, a soldier doesn't make a lot of money these days

Which country do you think has the largest army in the world today?

I think ... has the largest army in the world today

What do we call the clothes that a soldier wears?

We call the clothes that a soldier wears a uniform

222 Do most children wear uniforms at school in your country?

Yes, most children wear uniforms at school in my country ~ No, most children don't wear uniforms at school in my country

build

Is it cheap to build a large house in the country?

No, it isn't cheap to build a large house in the country; it's expensive

fill

Do you fill your stomach completely when you eat?

Yes, I fill my stomach completely when I eat ~ No, I don't fill my stomach completely when I eat

contain

About how many pages does this book contain?

This book contains about ... pages

art   artist

Are you very good at art?

Yes, I'm very good at art ~ No, I'm not very good at art

Was Picasso a writer or an artist?

Picasso was an artist

feel   too much

Do you always feel in good health?

Yes, I always feel in good health ~ No, I don't always feel in good health

223 Do you feel bad if you eat too much?

Yes, I feel bad if I eat too much

Do you feel sad in good weather?

No, I don't feel sad in good weather; I feel happy in good weather

See Chart 6

middle   centre

What part of the square's this?

It's the top of the square; it's the bottom of the square; it's the side of the square; it's the middle of the square

Where's the letter E?

The letter E's in the top right-hand corner of the square

Where's the letter I?

The letter I's in the bottom left-hand corner of the square

Where's the letter U?	The letter U's in the middle of the square
Do people drive their cars in the middle of the road?	No, people don't drive their cars in the middle of the road; in most countries they drive them on the right-hand side of the road
What's another word for "middle"?	Another word for "middle" is "centre"
Is there anything in the centre of this room?	Yes, there's something in the centre of this room ~ No, there isn't anything in the centre of this room

224   sure

What's your name?	My name's ...
Are you sure?	Yes, I'm sure
How many ears have you?	I've two ears
Are you sure?	Yes, I'm sure

request

Do we generally say "please" in English at the beginning of a request?	No, we don't generally say please in English at the beginning of a request; we say it at the end of a request
Is it polite not to say "please" when we make a request?	No, it isn't polite not to say "please" when we make a request; it's impolite

neither ... nor

Is this a desk or a chair?	No, it's neither a desk nor a chair; it's a door
Are there a hundred chairs in this room or a thousand chairs?	No, there are neither a hundred chairs in this room nor a thousand chairs; there are ... chairs in this room
Are you Mr Brown or Mr Smith?	No, I'm neither Mr Brown nor Mr Smith; I'm ...

Are you always willing to help other people?   Yes, I'm always
willing to help other people ~ No,
I'm not always willing to help other people

Are you willing to give me all the money you have in your pocket (or bag) at the moment?   No, I'm not willing
to give you all the money I have
in my pocket (or bag) at the moment

226 **Irregular verbs** (continued)

film			pronunciation		
leave	–	left	read	–	read
smell	–	smelt	meet	–	met
learn	–	learnt	feel	–	felt
send	–	sent	hear	–	heard
know	–	knew	hold	–	held
hang	–	hung	bring	–	brought
buy	–	bought	go	–	went
shake	–	shook	say	–	said
think	–	thought	teach	–	taught

What's the past of "leave"?

The past of leave is "left"

What time did you leave home to come here today?

I left home at ... to come here today

What's the past of "smell"?

The past of smell is "smelt"

Did your lunch smell bad yesterday?

No, my lunch didn't smell bad yesterday; it smelt good

227 Did you learn any new words last week?

Yes, I learnt some new words last week

Did you send any emails to your friends last month?

Yes, I sent some emails to my friends last month

Did you know me two weeks ago?

Yes, I knew you two weeks ago

Did that picture hang on the wall last lesson?

Yes, that picture hung on the wall last lesson

Did we read these books last week?

Yes, we read these books last week

Who was the last person you met before coming to the school?

... was the last person I
met before coming to the school

Did you feel cold last summer?

No, I didn't feel cold
last summer; I felt hot

Did you hear me say "Good morning" (or afternoon etc.) to you at the beginning of the lesson?

Yes, I heard you say "Good ..."
to us at the beginning of the lesson

What did I hold in my hand last lesson?

You held your
pen in your hand last lesson

What did you bring with you to the lesson today?

I brought my books
with me to the lesson today

Where did you buy your clothes from?

I bought my clothes from ...
(or "a clothes shop")

Did you go to the pub last month?

Yes, I went to the pub last month ~
No, I didn't go to the pub last month

Who was the last person you shook hands with?

... was the last
person I shook hands with

What did I say to you at the end of the last lesson?

You said "Goodbye"
to us at the end of the last lesson

228 Did you think the last film you saw was a good one?

Yes, I thought the
last film I saw was a good one ~ No, I didn't think
the last film I saw was a good one; I thought it was bad

Did you think English pronunciation was difficult when you first began studying English?

Yes, I thought English
pronunciation was difficult
when I first began studying English

Did your parents teach you to wash and dress when you were a child?

Yes, my parents taught me to
wash and dress when I was a child

bicycle	**motorbike**	**bike**

Which is quicker: a bicycle or a motorbike?

A motorbike
is quicker than a bicycle

What's a bike?

A bike is either a bicycle or a motorbike

mistake

Did you make any mistakes in your last dictation?   Yes, I made some
mistakes in my last dictation

Do you ever mistake the word "walk" for "work" when you hear it?
Yes, I sometimes mistake the
word "walk" for "work" when I hear it

listen	hear	news

radio	radio station	all the time

What am I doing?   You're listening to something

I am listening, but can I hear anything?   Yes, you can
hear something

What can I hear?   You can hear the cars in the street etc.

Did you hear the news on the radio yesterday?   Yes, I heard the news
on the radio yesterday ~ No, I didn't
hear the news on the radio yesterday

How often do they give the news on the radio each day?   They give
the news about ... times
(or every hour etc.) on the radio each day

Do you listen to the same radio station all the time?   Yes, I listen to the
same radio station all the time ~ No, I
don't listen to the same radio station all the time

ill	well	a cold	medicine

Do you ever feel ill?   Yes, I sometimes feel ill

Do you take medicine when you feel ill?   Yes, I take medicine when I
feel ill ~ No, I don't take medicine when I feel ill

When was the last time you felt ill?   The last time I felt ill was ...

What's the opposite of "ill"?   The opposite of "ill" is "well"

Do people feel well when they have a cold?   No, people don't feel well
when they have a cold; they feel ill

favourite	**thirsty**	**programme**

Are you thirsty at the moment?

Yes, I'm thirsty at the moment
~ No, I'm not thirsty at the moment

What's your favourite drink apart from water when you feel very thirsty?

My favourite drink apart from
water when I feel very thirsty is ...

What's your favourite television programme?

My favourite
television programme is ...

sell	**supermarket**

What's the opposite of the verb "to buy"?

The opposite
of the verb "to buy" is "to sell"

In what kind of shops do they generally sell umbrellas?

They generally
sell umbrellas in clothes shops

Do they sell food in clothes shops?

No, they don't sell food in clothes
shops; they sell it in supermarkets

Is there a supermarket in the centre of this town?

Yes, there's a
supermarket in the centre of this town ~ No,
there isn't a supermarket in the centre of this town

 Dictation 23 ·

231

They go to bed at ten/ and get up at seven./ They sleep nine hours./ I love both tennis and basketball,/ but don't play either well./ He hates going to the shops/ at the weekend./ Count up to ten, please./ He has the least money./ The word "mine"/ is a possessive pronoun./ "On" is a preposition./ "Break" is an irregular verb./ That phone is excellent./ What does the word "stomach" mean?/ "Go!" is imperative./ The names of five vegetables are/ potatoes, tomatoes,/ onions, carrots and peas.

Do Revision Exercise 15

232   **lots of**   **away**   **tell**

What can we say instead of "a lot of"?

We can say "lots of" instead of "a lot of"

If you have lots of work to do and a friend talks to you all the time, what do you tell him to do?

If I have lots of work to do and a friend talks to me all the time, I tell him to go away

Did you go away for your holidays last summer?

Yes, I went away for my holidays last summer ~ No, I didn't go away for my holidays last summer

Where did you go? Did you like it?

I went to ...

Do you ever give any money away?

Yes, I sometimes give some money away ~ No, I never give any money away

Do you take this book away with you after the lesson?

No, I don't take that book away with me after the lesson

Why not?

Because it isn't mine

   business   **foreign**

Does this country do business with foreign countries?

Yes, this country does business with foreign countries

233   **rainy**   **sunny**   **cloudy**

Is Greece a rainy country?

No, Greece isn't a rainy country; it's a sunny country

Is it a sunny day today?

Yes, it's a sunny day today ~ No, it isn't a sunny day today

Was it a cloudy day yesterday?

Yes, it was a cloudy day yesterday ~ No, it wasn't a cloudy day yesterday

Do you think it will be a rainy day tomorrow?

Yes, I think it'll be a rainy day tomorrow ~ No, I don't think it'll be a rainy day tomorrow

nature

Do you think nature is always beautiful?

Yes, I think nature is always beautiful ~ No, I don't think nature is always beautiful

price

What is the price of a meal in a very cheap restaurant in the place where you live?

The price of a meal in a very cheap restaurant in the place where I live is about ...

bush

Is a bush higher (or taller) than a tree?

No, a bush isn't higher (or taller) than a tree; it's lower (or shorter) than a tree

234 worth · to be worth · value

What does it mean if I say "This book is worth £5"?

If you say that book is worth £5, it means that you can sell it for £5, or that it has a value of £5

How much did your watch cost?

My watch cost ...

When did you buy it?

I bought it ...

About how much do you think it's worth now?

I think it's worth about ... now

Are your shoes worth as much now as they were when you bought them?

No, my shoes aren't worth as much now as they were when I bought them; they're worth less now than they were when I bought them

How much do you think this is worth?

I think that's worth about ...

Worth + -ing (gerund)

If we say that something is 'worth doing', we mean that it is better to do it than not do it. For example, if you live in a very rainy country, it is worth buying an umbrella. If you live in a very sunny country, it is not worth buying an umbrella.

Do you think it's worth paying lots of money for clothes?

> Yes, I think it's worth paying lots of money for clothes ~ No, I don't think it's worth paying lots of money for clothes

235 Do you think it's worth studying the language of another country?

> Yes, I think it's worth studying the language of another country

Do you think it's worth buying an umbrella if you live in a country where it only rains about once a month?

> No, I don't think it's worth buying an umbrella if I live in a country where it only rains about once a month

Do you think it's worth taking an umbrella with you on a rainy day?

> Yes, I think it's worth taking an umbrella with me on a rainy day

hard   soft

What are the three meanings of the word "hard"?

> The three meanings of the word "hard" are "difficult", "very much", and the opposite of "soft"

Is Chinese an easy language to learn?

> No, Chinese isn't an easy language to learn; it's a hard language to learn

Is English grammar hard?

> No, English grammar isn't hard; it's easy

Do you work very hard?

> Yes, I work very hard ~ No, I don't work very hard; I work very little

Do you think you generally work harder than your parents?

> Yes, I think I generally work harder than my parents ~ No, I don't think I generally work harder than my parents; I think I work less than my parents (or less hard than my parents)

236 **Is my hand hard?**   No, your hand isn't hard; it's soft

Is the floor soft?   No, the floor isn't soft; it's hard

Dictation 24

I arrive at eight o'clock,/ study one hour,/ and leave at nine./ During the day/ we can see the sun in the sky,/ whilst during the night/ we can see the moon and the stars./ Paris is not by the sea,/ but inland./ He cut his finger;/ not once, not twice, but three times./ They cannot lift the table/ on their backs./ The four seasons are/ spring, summer, autumn and winter./ He does not follow the teacher/ into the room,/ but he precedes him.

LESSON 46

237 | **Future tense** | | **"Will" + infinitive without "to"** |

I	will eat	I'll	eat
you	will eat	you'll	eat
he	will eat	he'll	eat
she	will eat	she'll	eat
it	will eat	it'll	eat
we	will eat	we'll	eat
you	will eat	you'll	eat
they	will eat	they'll	eat

We form the future tense with the word "will" and the infinitive without "to". The future of "I go" is "I will go". The future of "you go" is "you will go". The complete future tense of the verb "to go" is "I will go", "you will go", "he will go", "she will go" etc.

What's the future of "I go"?

The future of "I go" is "I will go"

What's the future of "you go"?

The future of "you go" is "you will go"

What's the complete future of the verb "to go"?

The complete future of the verb "to go" is "I will go", "you will go" etc.

238 **The contraction of "I will" is "I'll"; the contraction of "you will" is "you'll" etc.**

What's the contraction of "I will"?

The contraction of "I will" is "I'll"

What's the contraction of "you will"?

The contraction of "you will" is "you'll"

What are the contractions of "he will", "she will" etc.?

The contractions of "he will",
"she will" etc. are "he'll", "she'll", etc.

in 3 months' time

The opposite of "3 months ago" is "in 3 months' time".

What's the opposite of 3 months ago?

The opposite of "3 months
ago" is "in 3 months' time"

Will I be here next week?

Yes, you'll be here next week

What time will I leave the classroom today?

You'll leave the
classroom at ... today

Will you go home after the lesson?

Yes, I'll go home
after the lesson

Where will you be in 6 months' time?

I'll be ... in 6 months' time

Will he be here next lesson?

Yes, he'll be here next lesson

Will it rain next year?

Yes, it'll rain next year

Will we be here in 3 weeks' time?

Yes, we'll be here in 3 weeks' time

239 Will they speak English during the next lesson?

Yes, they'll speak
English during the next lesson

won't   stay

The contraction of "I will not" is "I won't". The contraction of "you will not" is "you won't".

What's the contraction of "I will not"?

The contraction
of "I will not" is "I won't"

What's the contraction of "you will not"?

The contraction of "you
will not" is "you won't"

What are the contractions of "he will not", "she will not" etc.?

The contractions of "he will not",
"she will not" etc. are "he won't", "she won't" etc.

Will I go home in 2 minutes' time?

No, you won't go home in 2
minutes' time; you'll stay here

Will you be here in a hundred years' time?	No, I won't be here in a hundred years' time
Will he stay here after the lesson?	No, he won't stay here after the lesson; he'll ...
Will we live for a thousand years?	No, we won't live for a thousand years

240 Will they agree to give you all the money they have in their pockets if you ask them?

No, they won't agree to give me all the money they have in their pockets if I ask them

shall   suggestion

We use "shall" instead of "will" when we are making a suggestion with the pronoun "I" or "we". For example, we say "Shall I open the window?", "Shall we go to the cinema?" etc. We can also ask somebody for a suggestion with "shall". For example, we can ask "What shall I do?", "Where shall we go?" etc.

When do we use "shall" instead of "will"?	We use "shall" when we are making a suggestion with the pronoun "I" or "we"
Give me some examples, please.	Shall I open the window? Shall we go to the cinema?
Can we use "shall" to ask for a suggestion?	Yes, we can use "shall" to ask for a suggestion
Give me some examples, please.	What shall I do? Where shall we go?

public   in public   public holiday

Is this building open to the public?	No, this building isn't open to the public
How many public holidays are there in your country each year?	There are ... public holidays in my country each year

241 Do you like speaking in public?

Yes, I like speaking in public ~ No, I don't like speaking in public

show

Show me your book, please.

What are you doing?   I'm showing you my book

Can you show me the way to the station from here?   Yes, I can show
you the way to the station from here ~ No, I
can't show you the way to the station from here

kill   tiger

Do tigers kill other animals for food?   Yes, tigers kill
other animals for food

Do you like films in which lots of people get killed?   Yes, I like films in
which lots of people get killed ~ No, I
don't like films in which lots of people get killed

 *Do Revision Exercise 16*

LESSON 47

queen   **head**

Are there many countries in the world which have a queen as the head of the government?

No, there aren't
many countries in the world which
have a queen as the head of the government

blood

What colour's blood?

Blood's red

offer   **company**   **in company**

chocolate   **chocolates**

When you're eating chocolates in company, do you offer them round?

Yes, when I'm eating chocolates
in company, I offer them round ~ No, when I'm
eating chocolates in company, I don't offer them round

If I offer you a million pounds, will you take it?

Yes, if you offer me a
million pounds, I'll take it ~ No, if you
offer me a million pounds, I won't take it

life   **death**   **in the past**

What's the opposite of "life"?

The opposite of "life" is "death"

Do you think life is more pleasant for children or adults?

I think life
is more pleasant for ...

Do you think life is harder these days than it was in the past?

No, I don't think life is harder these
days than it was in the past; I think it's easier

In your country, what colour do you use for death?

In my country,
we use ... for death

Is death a pleasant subject to speak about? No, death isn't a pleasant subject to speak about

suggest   exercise

What do doctors suggest doing for a healthy life? Doctors suggest eating healthy food and getting lots of fresh air and exercise for a healthy life

Where do you suggest he/she goes for his/her holiday next year? I suggest he/she goes to … for his/her holiday next year

Tomorrow I'll buy a new shirt (or dress); what colour do you suggest I buy? I suggest you buy a … shirt (or dress)

If he/she wants to see a film tonight, which film do you suggest he/she sees? I suggest he/she sees …

What do you suggest I do this weekend? I suggest you … this weekend

244   tonight

What time will you go to bed tonight? I'll go to bed at … tonight

What will you do before going to bed tonight? I'll watch TV, read, go to the cinema etc. before going to bed tonight

tired   tired of

Are you tired at the moment? Yes, I'm tired at the moment ~ No, I'm not tired at the moment

What do you do when you feel tired? When I feel tired, I go to bed

Are you tired of studying? Yes, I'm tired of studying ~ No, I'm not tired of studying

turn   turn over

What am I doing? You're turning round

If you turn round, what will you see? If I turn round, I'll see a picture etc.

Can you turn completely round without standing up?　　　No, I can't
turn completely round without standing up

What am I doing?　　　You're turning over a page in your book

245　got

The past of "get" is "got".

What's the past of "get"?　　　The past of "get" is "got"

Where did you get your shoes?　　　I got my shoes
from ... (or "a shoe shop")

What time did you get here today?　　　I got here at ... today

Did you get to school early today?　　　Yes, I got to
school early today ~ No, I
didn't get to school early today

until　　　till

Will you be in this room until 10 o'clock this evening?
Yes, I'll be in this room until 10 o'clock this evening ~
No, I won't be in this room until 10 o'clock this evening

Do you want to live until you're a hundred years old?
Yes, I want to live until I'm a hundred years old ~
No, I don't want to live until I'm a hundred years old

Are supermarkets sometimes open till late at night?
Yes, supermarkets are sometimes open till late at night

again　　　too many

Will you come here again next week?　　　Yes, I'll come here again next
week ~ No, I won't come here again next week

246　Will I ask you the same questions again next lesson as I am asking you
now?　　　Yes, you'll ask us the same questions
again next lesson as you are asking us now

If we make too many mistakes in our dictations, do you think it's better to
do them again?　　　Yes, if we make too
many mistakes in our dictations,
I think it's better to do them again

duration

What's the duration of a lesson in this school?

> The duration of a lesson in this school is ... minutes

What's the duration of a game of football?

> The duration of a game of football is 90 minutes

there will be   there'll be

Will there be anything on TV tonight?

> Yes, there'll
> be something on TV tonight

Will there be any pictures hanging on these walls next lesson?

> Yes, there'll be some pictures
> hanging on these walls next lesson

Will there be a chair on the table next lesson?

> No, there won't be a
> chair on the table next lesson

Will there be anybody sitting on the floor next lesson?

> No, there
> won't be anybody
> sitting on the floor next lesson

247   *Dictation 25*

"New" we use for things,/ whereas "young" we use for people./ That shop is older than ours./ Christmas and Easter/ are the two most important holidays/ of the year./ When our stomachs are empty,/ we must eat,/ but not when they are full./ He doesn't like the subject of mathematics/ very much./ On a cold morning,/ he sometimes dresses before washing./ Juice, geography, fruit, telephone, apple./ Finland is/ one of the coldest countries/ in the world,/ whilst India is/ one of the hottest./ England is cool./ Italy is warm./ Her flat is near our house./ She lives in the first block.

LESSON 48

248   **newspaper**   **magazine**   **popular**

Which newspaper do you read?   I read ...

Which is one of the most popular newspapers in this country?

The ... is one of the most
popular newspapers in this country

Do you often read magazines?   Yes, I often read magazines ~
No, I don't often read magazines

sold

What's the past of "sell"?   The past of "sell" is "sold"

Which shop sold you your shoes?   ... sold me my shoes

coal

What do we use to make a fire?   We use wood, paper,
coal etc. to make a fire

What colour's coal?   Coal's black

decide   **menu**

In a restaurant, what do we look at to decide what we want to eat?

In a restaurant, we look at a
menu to decide what we want to eat

249   Did you decide to study English, or did somebody in your family decide
for you?   I decided to study English;
nobody in my family decided for me ~
Somebody in my family decided for me

explain

Explain the difference between the present continuous and the present simple, please.

The difference between the present continuous and the present simple is that we use the present continuous for an action we are doing now, whereas we use the present simple for an action we do generally

What's he doing?

He's explaining the difference between the present continuous and the present simple

heaven   hell

Which place in the world do you think is most like heaven?

I think ... is most like heaven

What's the opposite of "heaven"?

The opposite of "heaven" is "hell"

book

Is it a good idea to book a table before going to a very popular restaurant?

Yes, it's a good idea to book a table before going to a very popular restaurant

try   try hard   possible   impossible

Do you always try hard to answer the questions I ask you?

Yes, I always try hard to answer the questions you ask me

250 Are you always willing to try anything new?

Yes, I'm always willing to try anything new ~ No, I'm not always willing to try anything new

Do some people sometimes try to do the impossible?

Yes, some people sometimes try to do the impossible

quiet   noisy

Are cities quiet places to live in?

No, cities aren't quiet places to live in; they're noisy places

Is village life noisy?

No, village life isn't noisy; it's quiet

Which do you think's the noisiest street in this town? I think … is the noisiest street in this town

Are motorbikes quieter than bicycles? No, motorbikes aren't quieter than bicycles; they're noisier than bicycles

sorry	pleased	I'm sorry

Are you sorry when the winter ends? Yes, I'm sorry when the winter ends ~ No, I'm not sorry when the winter ends; I'm pleased

Will you be sorry if it's a sunny day tomorrow? No, I won't be sorry if it's a sunny day tomorrow; I'll be pleased

What do we say to people when we do something wrong? We say "I'm sorry" to people when we do something wrong

251 had

The past of "have" is "had".

What's the past of "have"? The past of "have" is "had"

What did I have in my hand last lesson? You had a pen in your hand last lesson

What did you have for your breakfast this morning? I had some coffee, some bread etc. for my breakfast this morning

What did he/she have for his/her breakfast this morning? He/She had some … for his/her breakfast this morning

Did we have any shoes on our feet yesterday? Yes, we had some shoes on our feet yesterday

Did they have any money in their pockets (or bags) last lesson? Yes, they had some money in their pockets (or bags) last lesson

could   baby

The past of "can" is "could".

What's the past of "can"?   The past of "can" is "could"

Could you speak English fifteen years ago?   No, I couldn't speak
English fifteen years ago

Could you write your name when you were a baby of six months old?
No, I couldn't write my name
when I was a baby of six months old

Could you read when you were a little baby?   No, I couldn't read
when I was a little baby

perhaps   maybe   a friend of yours

Do you think maybe it'll rain later?   Yes, I think maybe
it'll rain later ~ No, I don't think it'll rain later

Do you think perhaps you'll meet a friend of yours on your way home
after the lesson?   Yes, I think perhaps
I'll meet a friend of mine on my way home
after the lesson ~ No, I don't think I'll meet a
friend of mine on my way home after the lesson

Do you think maybe you'll go to the cinema next month?
Yes, I think maybe I'll go to the cinema next month
~ No, I don't think I'll go to the cinema next month

sweet

Do you like sweet food?   Yes, I like sweet food ~
No, I don't like sweet food

Did you eat a lot of sweets when you were a child?
Yes, I ate a lot of sweets when I was a child
~ No, I didn't eat a lot of sweets when I was a child

I can't taste the difference/ between these two wines./ An hour is divided into minutes./ I can walk no further;/ I must rest./ Send the children/ into the other room;/ I want to read./ I get up early in summer,/ but later in winter./ I go to bed/ earlier than my father./ It isn't dark in this room/ when the sun is shining./ A millionaire/ is a very rich person./ Ash, university, shallow,/ complicated, reply./ The message we often write/ inside a Christmas card is/ "Merry Christmas and a Happy New Year".

Do Revision Exercise 17

LESSON 49

spoken   **written**

Do we generally use contractions in spoken or written English?

We generally use contractions in spoken English

Do you think it's easier to understand written English or spoken English?

I think it's easier to understand ... English

book will	book'll
tomorrow will	tomorrow'll
light will	light'll
Mr Smith will	Mr Smith'll
who will	who'll
what will	what'll

The contraction of "book will" is "book'll"; "tomorrow will – tomorrow'll"; "Mr Smith will – Mr Smith'll"; "who will – who'll"; "what will – what'll" etc.

What's the contraction of "book will"?

The contraction of "book will" is "book'll"

Tomorrow will; the light will; the door will; who will; what will

tomorrow'll; the light'll; the door'll; who'll; what'll

255 **We generally use contractions when we speak, but we don't use them if they are difficult to pronounce. For example, we say "pen'll" but not "pencil'll".**

Do we always use contractions in English?

No, we don't always use contractions in English

When don't we use contractions?

We don't use contractions when they are difficult to pronounce

Do you think tomorrow'll be a cloudy day?   Yes, I think
tomorrow'll be a cloudy day ~ No, I don't think
tomorrow'll be a cloudy day; I think it'll be sunny

Will that picture be hanging on the wall next lesson?   Yes, that picture'll
be hanging on the wall next lesson

Will the door be the same colour next week as it is this week?
Yes, the door'll be the same
colour next week as it is this week

Will Mr Brown be here next lesson?   Yes, Mr Brown'll
be here next lesson

spell

How do you spell your name?   I spell my name ...

communicate   easily

Do you prefer to communicate with your friends by phoning or texting?
I prefer to communicate
with my friends by ...

Do you think it's easier to communicate in spoken or written English?
I think it's easier to
communicate in ... English

256 Can you communicate very complicated ideas easily in English?
No, I can't communicate very
complicated ideas easily in English

hadn't

The negative of "had" is "hadn't".

What's the negative of "had"?   The negative of "had" is "hadn't"

Different forms of "have"

The common ways of asking a question with the verb "have" are:

   1) Do you have a pen?

   2) Have you got a pen?

In the past tense, it is the same. We can say:

   1) Did you have a pen?

   2) Had you got a pen?

The most common way of asking a question with the verb "have" in the past is "Did you have ...?"

What are the common ways of asking a question with the verb "to have"?

        The common ways of asking a question with the verb "to have" are 1) Do you have a pen? and 2) Have you got a pen?

257 What are the common ways for the past tense?

        The common ways for the past tense are 1) Did you have a pen? 2) Had you got a pen?

Which is the most common way of asking a question with the verb 'have' in the past?

        The most common way of asking a question with the verb 'have' in the past is "Did you have ...?"

Did you have your book with you last lesson?

        Yes, I had my book with me last lesson

Did I have a hat on my head last lesson?

        No, you didn't have a hat on your head last lesson

Had I got any money in my hand last lesson?

        No, you hadn't got any money in your hand last lesson

Did I have my feet on the table last lesson?

        No, you didn't have your feet on the table last lesson

practise	**practice**	**sport**

Did you practise your English after you left school yesterday?

Yes, I practised my English after I left school yesterday ~ No, I didn't practise my English after I left school yesterday

Is it easier to become good at a sport if you get lots of practice?

Yes, it's easier to become good at a sport if you get lots of practice

258 What's the difference between the noun "practice" and the verb "practise"?

The difference between the noun "practice" and the verb "practise" is that we spell the noun with a "c" and we spell the verb with an "s"

would like

What's a polite way of communicating that you want something?

A polite way of communicating that you want something is to say "I would like ..."

Give me an example, please.

I would like a cup of tea; I would like to watch that TV programme

What can we say when we offer something to somebody?

When we offer something to somebody, we can say "Would you like ...?"

Give me an example, please.

Would you like a cup of tea? Would you like to go to the cinema?

visit   Australia

Can we learn a lot by visiting different countries?

Yes, we can learn a lot by visiting different countries

Did you visit any new places last month?

Yes, I visited some new places last month ~ No, I didn't visit any new places last month

Would you like to visit Australia in the future?

Yes, I would like to visit Australia in the future ~ No, I wouldn't like to visit Australia in the future

The difference between "use" /juːz/ and "use" /juːs/ is that "use" /juːz/ is the verb whereas "use" /juːs/ is the noun.

What's the difference between "use" /juːz/ and "use" /juːs/?

The difference between "use" /juːz/ and "use" /juːs/ is that "use" /juːz/ is the verb, whereas "use" /juːs/ is the noun

What's the use of a pen?   The use of a pen is for writing

What's the use in studying languages?   The use in studying languages is to make it possible for us to speak to people from other countries

Dictation 27

We watch a game of football,/ but look at a photograph./ He speaks better than I do./ I am the worst/ in the class,/ while he is the best./ I buy my soap/ from that shop/ besides shampoo./ I forgot my camera,/ so I took the photos/ with my mobile instead./ I know I can hold/ a simple conversation in English./ Poor, story, hill,/ farm, laugh, rich,/ soldier, stop, castle,/ enemy./ Not every student is quick;/ some are quick/ and some are slow./ I'm always sad/ when it rains on Sunday.

LESSON 50

260 **therefore**

Give me an example of the word "therefore", please.　　I want to learn
English well. Therefore, I must study.

sound	**traffic**	**silent**

Can you hear the sound of my pen on the table?　　Yes, I can hear the
sound of your pen on the table

Can you hear the sound of traffic at the moment?　　Yes, I can hear
the sound of traffic at the moment
~ No, I can't hear the sound of traffic at the moment

Do you think the English language sounds pleasant?　　Yes, I think the
English language sounds pleasant ~ No, I
don't think the English language sounds pleasant

Do I sound angry at the moment?　　No, you don't
sound angry at the moment

Is your house completely silent at night or can you hear street noise?
My house is completely
silent at night ~ My house isn't
completely silent at night; I can hear street noise

a	**the** /ðə/ before a consonant sound
an	**the** /ði:/ before a vowel sound

261 **The difference between "a" and "an" is that we use "a" before a
consonant sound whereas we use "an" before a vowel sound. For
example, we say "a book" because the word "book" starts with the
sound /b/, a consonant sound. We say "an apple" because the word
"apple" starts with the sound /æ/, a vowel sound.**

What's the difference between "a" and "an"?   The difference
between "a" and "an" is
that we use "a" before a consonant sound,
whereas we use "an" before a vowel sound

Give me an example of each, please.   "a book"; "an apple"

The difference between "the" /ðə/ and "the"/ði:/ is the same; we use "the" /ðə/ before a consonant sound whereas we use "the"/ði:/ before a vowel sound.

Give me an example of "the" /ðə/.   The /ðə/ chair is red
Give me an example of "the" /ði:/.   The /ði:/ apple is red

The noun "use" starts with the letter "u", a vowel, but it starts with the sound /j/, a consonant sound. Therefore, we say "the /ðə/ use" and not "the /ði:/ use".

Why do we say "the /ðə/ use" and not "the /ði:/ use"?
We say "the /ðə/ use" and not "the /ði:/ use"
because the word "use" starts with a consonant sound

Remember, some words that begin with the letter "h" start with a vowel sound, because the "h" is silent. For example, we say "an hour" and not "a hour".

Is it right to say "a hour" or "an hour"?   It's right to say "an hour"

Why?   Because the letter "h" in the word "hour" is silent

---

262   **succeed   fail   examination (exam)**

take an examination   pass

Generally, after the verb "succeed", we use the word "in" and the gerund. For example, we say "succeed in going", "succeed in taking" etc.

Did you fail to answer the last question?   No, I didn't
fail to answer the last question; I
succeeded **in** answer**ing** the last question

If you try hard, do you think you'll succeed in learning English well?

Yes, if I try hard, I think I'll succeed in learning English well

What's the opposite of "to fail an exam"?

The opposite of "to fail an exam" is "to pass an exam"

Do you think you'll pass the stage exam at the end of this book?

Yes, I think I'll pass the stage exam at the end of this book

If you fail an examination do you always take it again?

Yes, if I fail an examination, I always take it again ~ No, if I fail an examination, I don't always take it again

Do people generally succeed in getting what they want if they try hard enough?

Yes, people generally succeed in getting what they want if they try hard enough

have to (= must)

"Have to" means the same as "must". We can say "I must go to school" or "I have to go to school". However, we cannot use "must" to speak about the past. Instead, we use "had to" and say "Yesterday, I had to go to school".

263 What can we say instead of "I must study"?

Instead of "I must study", we can say "I have to study"

Do you have to eat if you want to live?

Yes, I have to eat if I want to live

Did you have to get up early yesterday morning?

Yes, I had to get up early yesterday morning ~ No, I didn't have to get up early yesterday morning

Will you have to wait if you arrive too early for the next lesson?

Yes, I'll have to wait if I arrive too early for the next lesson

The negatives of "have to" and "must" have different meanings. "I don't have to do it"means that I can do it if I want, but it is not necessary. "I mustn't do it" means that it is bad or wrong to do it.

Which is it right to say: "You mustn't smoke in this building" or "You don't have to smoke in this building"?

It's right to say "You mustn't smoke in this building"

Which is it right to say: "I mustn't get up early on Saturday" or "I don't have to get up early on Saturday"?

It's right to say "I don't have to get up early on Saturday"

Must you study if you want to learn English?

Yes, I must study if I want to learn English

Must you study ten hours a day if you want to learn English?

No, I don't have to study ten hours a day if I want to learn English

 *Do Revision Exercise 18*

LESSON 51

worker	beginner	sleeper

writer	speaker

To form a noun from a verb we sometimes add the letters "er" to the verb. For example, we call a person who works a "worker"; we call a person who writes a "writer" etc.

How do we sometimes form a noun from a verb?
> We sometimes form a noun from a verb by adding the letters "er" to the verb

Give me some examples, please.
> eat – eater; walk – walker; speak – speaker

Are you a hard worker?
> Yes, I'm a hard worker ~ No, I'm not a hard worker; I work very little

Are you a complete beginner in English?
> No, I'm not a complete beginner in English; I began ...

Are you a heavy (or deep) sleeper?
> Yes, I'm a heavy sleeper ~ No, I'm not a heavy sleeper; I'm a light sleeper

Who's your favourite writer?
> My favourite writer is ...

hope

Do you hope you'll live a very long time?
> Yes, I hope I'll live a very long time ~ No, I don't hope I'll live a very long time

Do you think it's important to be positive about life and full of hope for the future?
> Yes, I think it's important to be positive about life and full of hope for the future

Do you hope the weather will be sunny tomorrow?
> Yes, I hope the weather will be sunny tomorrow

believe   planet

Do you believe everything people tell you?

No, I don't believe everything people tell me; some things I believe and some things I disbelieve

Do you believe there is life on other planets?

Yes, I believe there is life on other planets ~ No, I don't believe there is life on other planets

Do you believe it'll be possible in the future for people to live until they're two hundred years old?

Yes, I believe it'll be possible in the future for people to live until they're two hundred years old ~ No, I don't believe it'll be possible in the future for people to live until they're two hundred years old

do the shopping   go shopping   list

What's the difference between "to do the shopping" and "to go shopping"?

The difference between "to do the shopping" and "to go shopping" is that "to do the shopping" means to buy the things that are necessary for the house, such as food etc., whereas "to go shopping" means to visit shops generally

266 When you do the shopping, do you make a list before going to the supermarket?

Yes, when I do the shopping, I make a list before going to the supermarket ~ No, when I do the shopping, I don't make a list before going to the supermarket

Do you ever go shopping and come home with nothing?

Yes, I sometimes go shopping and come home with nothing ~ No, I never go shopping and come home with nothing; I always buy something

smile

Do people generally smile when they're unhappy?

No, people don't generally smile when they're unhappy

Does good news put a smile on your face?

Yes, good news puts a smile on my face

tax

Do you have to pay a tax to the government if you buy a foreign car?

Yes, I have to pay a tax to the
government if I buy a foreign car ~ No, I don't
have to pay a tax to the government if I buy a foreign car

The three forms of a verb   **Past participle**

Present	Past	Past participle
walk	walked	walked
cut	cut	cut
sit	sat	sat
see	saw	seen
present:		I **see** him every week
past:		I **saw** him last week
past participle:		I have **seen** him this week

Generally speaking, each verb in English has three forms that you must learn:

   1) the present

   2) the past

   3) the past participle

For example, the three forms of the verb "to see" are "see, saw, seen", where "see" is the present, "saw" is the past, and "seen" is the past participle.

What are the three forms of an English verb?

The three forms of
an English verb are the present,
the past and the past participle

Give me an example, please.

see, saw, seen –
I see him every week;
I saw him last week; I have seen him this week

With regular verbs, the 2nd and 3rd forms are the same - for example, "kill, killed, killed". With irregular verbs, sometimes all the forms are the same – for example, "put, put, put"; sometimes two forms are the same – for example, "come, came, come"; and sometimes all three forms are different – for example, "give, gave, given".

What are the three forms of "kill"?

The three forms of "kill" are "kill, killed, killed"

What are the three forms of "put"?

The three forms of "put" are "put, put, put"

What are the three forms of "come"?

The three forms of "come" are "come, came, come"

What are the three forms of "give"?

The three forms of "give" are "give, gave, given"

Dictation 28

The past tense of the verb "to be" is/ "I was", "you were" etc./ They were sitting together/ three lessons ago; now they sit apart./ A road generally connects two towns,/ whereas a street is in a town./ I cannot walk in a straight line/ after drinking lots of whisky;/ I walk crooked./ When I go on holiday,/ I generally take a lot of photos./ "Ever" is positive/ and "never" is negative. When the weather is cold/ and there is snow,/ we cover our bodies/ with a lot of clothes.

LESSON 52

cat   **dog**   **result**   **lucky**

Which do you prefer: cats or dogs?

> I prefer ...

What is often the result of putting a cat and a dog together?

> The result of putting a cat and a dog together is often a lot of noise

Do people in your country think it's lucky to see a black cat?

> Yes, people in my country think it's lucky to see a black cat ~ No, people in my country don't think it's lucky to see a black cat; they think it's unlucky

destroy   **document**

Do you ever destroy documents that you receive from your bank?

> Yes, I sometimes destroy documents that I receive from my bank

Can a fire destroy a building?

> Yes, a fire can destroy a building

been   **Scotland**

The past participle of the verb "to be" is "been".

What's the past participle of the verb "to be"?

> The past participle of the verb "to be" is "been"

Have you been to the cinema this week?

> Yes, I've been to the cinema this week ~ No, I haven't been to the cinema this week

Have you ever been to Scotland?

> Yes, I've been to Scotland ~ No, I've never been to Scotland

Have you been to see the film ...?

> Yes, I've been to see the film ... ~ No, I haven't been to see the film ...

crime **guilty** **innocent**

against the law

What's a crime?
A crime is an action which is against the law

If I take something from a shop without paying, am I guilty of a crime?
Yes, if you take something from a shop without paying, you're guilty of a crime

What's the opposite of "guilty"?
The opposite of "guilty" is "innocent"

Do you always feel guilty when you do something wrong?
Yes, I always feel guilty when I do something wrong ~
No, I don't always feel guilty when I do something wrong

Is there very much crime in the town where you live?
Yes, there's a lot of crime in the town where I live
~ No, there isn't very much crime in the town where I live

Present perfect

"Have" + past participle (3rd form)

I have eaten **experience**

We form the present perfect with the verb "have" and the past participle. For example, we say "I have arrived" or "She has written".

271 The present perfect has three common uses:

1) We use it to talk about our experiences. If I say "I have eaten Chinese food", it means I have experience of "eating Chinese food". If I say "I have been to Paris", it means that I have experience of "being in Paris".

Do we use the present perfect to talk about our experiences?
Yes, we use the present perfect to talk about our experiences

Have you eaten Spanish food?
Yes, I have eaten Spanish food
~ No, I haven't eaten Spanish food

Have you visited Paris?

> Yes, I have visited Paris
> ~ No, I haven't visited Paris

Have you ever worked on a farm?

> Yes, I have worked on a farm
> ~ No, I have never worked on a farm

for   up to now

2) We also use the present perfect to talk about the duration of an action up to now. If I say "I have lived here for three years", it means that I'm living here now and I started living here three years ago.

Do we also use the present perfect to talk about the duration of an action up to now?

> Yes, we also use the
> present perfect to talk about
> the duration of an action up to now

How long have you lived in this town/city?

> I have lived
> in this town/city for ...

Have you studied English for more than six months?

> Yes, I have
> studied English for more than
> six months ~ No, I haven't studied English
> for more than six months; I have only studied it for ...

272   **3) We can also use the present perfect to talk about the result now of a past action. For example, "I have eaten too much" means that I feel bad (or guilty) now. "She has arrived" means that she is here now.**

Do we also use the present perfect to talk about the result now of a past action?

> Yes, we also use the
> present perfect to talk about
> the result now of a past action

Have you eaten too much today?

> Yes, I have eaten too much today ~
> No, I haven't eaten too much today

Has everybody come to the lesson today?

> Yes, everybody has
> come to the lesson today ~ No,
> not everybody has come to the lesson today

too many	too much	excessive

"Too many" and "too much" mean an excessive number or quantity, and therefore not a good thing. We use "too many" and "too much" with nouns, but with adjectives and adverbs we only use the word "too". For example, we say "too many cars" and "too much food", but we say "too short" and "too quickly".

What do "too many" and "too much" mean?　　　　　　"Too many" and "too much" mean an excessive number or quantity, and therefore not a good thing

Do children feel ill if they eat too many sweets?　　　　Yes, children feel ill if they eat too many sweets

Do you agree there are too many people in the world with too little food to eat?　　　　Yes, I agree there are too many people in the world with too little food to eat

273　Are you too short to touch the ceiling?　　Yes, I'm too short to touch the ceiling

Do you think a millionaire has too much money?
　　　　　　　　Yes, I think a millionaire has too much money
　　　　　　~ No, I don't think a millionaire has too much money

We can also use "too much" after a verb. For example, "If I eat too much, I feel bad".

If people eat too much, do they feel bad?　　　　　　Yes, if people eat too much, they feel bad

If you work too much, do you feel tired all the time?　　Yes, if I work too much, I feel tired all the time

 *Dictation 29*

We can sit at the corner/ of a square table,/ but we can't sit at the corner/ of a round one/ because, like a circle,/ a round table has no corners./ When she goes on holiday,/ she sends postcards/ to all her relations./ This method we are using/ is called the Callan Method./ The cinema was completely full./ He doesn't know/ if he will go to church tomorrow;/ he says/ it depends on the weather./ He'll text me or email me/ in the morning./ Business, foreign, nature,/ price, bush.

 *Do Revision Exercise 19*

274   **age**   **marry**   **get married**

At what age did you begin school?

> I began school
> at the age of ...

Which do you think is the best age for a person to get married?

> I think the best age for a
> person to get married is about ...

Which do you think was the best age in history to live in?

> I think ... was
> the best age in history to live in

Do people sometimes marry too young?

> Yes, people sometimes
> marry too young

average

How much does the average meal cost in the average restaurant in the place where you live?

> The average meal
> costs about ... in the average
> restaurant in the place where I live

What's the average number of hours a day that people work in this country?

> The average number of hours
> a day that people work in this country is about ...

About how many floors has the average building in this street got?

> The average building in
> this street's got about ... floors

275   **thick**   **thin**

Is this piece of paper thick?

> No, that piece of
> paper isn't thick; it's thin

Is your book thinner than the glass in the window?

> No, my book
> isn't thinner than the
> glass in the window; it's thicker

big   little

What words can we use instead of the words "large" and "small"?

> We can use the words "big" and "little"
> instead of the words "large" and "small"

Switzerland

Generally, we use "small" instead of "little" to form the comparative and superlative; we say "smaller" and "smallest" and not "littler" and "littlest", because they are easier to pronounce.

Do we generally say "littler" and "littlest"?

> No, we don't generally
> say "littler" and "littlest"

What do we use instead?

> We use "smaller" and "smallest" instead

Why?

> Because they're easier to pronounce

Is Switzerland a bigger country than India?

> No, Switzerland isn't a
> bigger country than India;
> it's a smaller country than India

276 Is this a little room we're in?

> Yes, this is a little
> room we're in ~ No, this isn't a
> little room we're in; it's a big room

purse   wallet   usually

What's the difference between a purse and a wallet?

> The difference between a purse and
> a wallet is that women generally have
> purses and men generally have wallets

What does a man carry in his wallet?

> A man carries his cash
> and cards in his wallet

lose   find   policeman

Do you ever lose your money?

> Yes, I sometimes lose my
> money ~ No, I never lose my money

If you lose your way in a large city, what do you do?

> If I lose my way
> in a large city, I ask a policeman

Which do you think it's worse to lose, your keys or your purse/wallet?

> I think it's worse to lose my ...

What's the opposite of the verb "to lose"?

> The opposite of the verb "to lose" is "to find"

If you find something in the street, what do you do with it?

> If I find something in the street, I ...

How do you feel if you lose something and then find it again?

> I feel happy if I lose something and then find it again

277 "Find" + somebody/something + adjective

Instead of saying "I think English is easy", we can say "I find English easy". Instead of "I think John is impolite", we can say "I find John impolite".

Do you find English easy to learn?

> Yes, I find English easy to learn ~ No, I don't find English easy to learn; I find it difficult

Do you find maps difficult to read?

> Yes, I find maps difficult to read ~ No, I don't find maps difficult to read; I find them easy to read

to be angry

"Make" + somebody/something + adjective

Do you get angry very easily?

> Yes, I get angry very easily ~ No, I don't get angry very easily

What kind of things make you angry?

> The kind of things that make me angry are when things go wrong, when people are making too much noise etc.

What do you do when you're angry?

> When I'm angry, I go for a walk, I say nothing etc.

Do you feel hungry at the moment?

> Yes, I feel hungry at the moment ~ No, I don't feel hungry at the moment

What do you do when you feel hungry?

> I eat when I feel hungry

Which do you prefer: fish or meat?   I prefer ...

Can you swim?   Yes, I can swim ~ No, I can't swim

What does it mean "to swim like a fish"?   "To swim like a fish"
                                                     means to be a strong swimmer

Do you prefer swimming in the sea or in a swimming pool?
                                                          I prefer swimming in ...

What do we call the two ends of a swimming pool?   We call the two
                                                     ends of a swimming pool
                                                     the shallow end and the deep end

 Dictation 30

There are nearly always/ a lot of clouds/ in the sky,/ and sometimes it rains./ "Quick" is an adjective;/ "quickly" is an adverb./ I often forget people's names./ However, I rarely forget/ a person's face./ I remember that/ the plural of wife is wives./ Excuse me,/ can you repeat the question please?/ We say "over"/ when there is no contact/ between the two objects,/ or when one object/ completely covers the other./ They're both very quick writers./ He does not understand the idea exactly./ He decided to explain everything/ to his friends and relatives.

. . . .

279 | **dream – dreamt – dreamt** | **nightmare**

Do you dream very much at night?

Yes, I dream a lot at night ~ No, I don't dream very much at night

What do we call a bad dream?

We call a bad dream a nightmare

What are the three forms of "dream"?

The three forms of "dream" are "dream, dreamt, dreamt"

What did you dream about last night?

I dreamt about ... last night

garden

Have you got a garden at home?

Yes, I've got a garden at home ~ No, I haven't got a garden at home

refuse

Do you ever refuse to help other people?

Yes, I sometimes refuse to help other people ~ No, I never refuse to help other people

separate

Do you write your dictations in a separate book from your other books?

Yes, I write my dictations in a separate book from my other books ~ No, I don't write my dictations in a separate book from my other books

280 Do you live in a separate house from your parents?

Yes, I live in a separate house from my parents ~ No, I don't live in a separate house from my parents; I live in the same house

lovely

Give me an example of the word "lovely", please.

> I had a lovely holiday last year. She's a lovely person. The weather's lovely today.

Keep   continue

The verb keep has many different meanings. Some of them are:

continue (keep + –ing)

Will you keep studying English until you die?

> Yes, I'll keep studying English until I die ~ No, I won't keep studying English until I die

Do you agree it's very bad for the health to keep eating after our stomachs are completely full?

> Yes, I agree it's very bad for the health to keep eating after our stomachs are completely full

have in a place

Do you keep your money in your pocket, or do you use a purse or wallet?

> I keep my money in my pocket ~ I don't keep my money in my pocket; I use a purse/wallet

not give away

Do you keep books after you've read them?

> Yes, I keep books after I've read them ~ No, I don't keep books after I've read them

stay

What's the best way to keep warm on a cold day?

> The best way to keep warm on a cold day is to wear a thick coat

one	you	we	they	mean

in general		necessarily		in particular

ticket

When we use the words "one", "you", "we" and "they", we sometimes mean people in general. The word "they" means other people and not us. For example, we say:

"If <u>one</u> goes to the cinema, one must buy a ticket", or

"If <u>you</u> go to the cinema, you must buy a ticket", or

"If <u>we</u> go to the cinema, we must buy a ticket".

As an example of "they", we can say "They don't sell food at a clothes shop".

When I say "If you want to go to the cinema, you have to buy a ticket", I don't necessarily mean you in particular, but people in general. We generally use the word "you" more than "one" or "we".

282 What do we sometimes mean when we use the words "one", "you", "we" and "they"?

> When we use the words "one", "you", "we" and "they" we sometimes mean people in general

In the sentence "If you want to go the cinema, you have to buy a ticket", what does the word "you" mean?

> In the sentence "If you want to go to the cinema, you have to buy a ticket", the word "you" doesn't necessarily mean me in particular, but people in general

Which do we generally use the most: "one", "you" or "we"?

> We generally use "you" the most

What must you do if you want to speak a language well?

> You must study a lot, and repeat, repeat and repeat, if you want to speak a language well

What do you have to do if you want to stay healthy?

> If you want to stay healthy, you have to eat healthy food, sleep well and do exercise

What must you do if you want to remember something well?

You must repeat often if you
want to remember something well

Where can we buy a drink when we're thirsty?

We can buy a drink
from a bar when we're thirsty

Which country must we go to if we want to hear people speaking Greek?

We must go to Greece if we
want to hear people speaking Greek

What does one do when one is hungry?

One eats when one is hungry

Do they sell drinks at most cinemas?

Yes, they sell drinks
at most cinemas

283 Do Revision Exercise 20

284
Present perfect	Past simple
before/up to now	specific past time
he has lived here for two months	he came here two months ago

The difference between the present perfect and the past simple is that we use the present perfect when we are thinking about time before or up to now, whereas we use the past simple when we are thinking about a specific past time. For example, "I have been here for twenty minutes; I arrived here twenty minutes ago".

What's the difference between the present perfect and the past simple?

> The difference between the present perfect and the past simple is that we use the present perfect when we are thinking about time before or up to now, whereas we use the past simple when we are thinking about a specific past time

Give me an example of each, please.

> I have been here for twenty minutes; I arrived here twenty minutes ago

Has the spring (or summer etc.) ended?

> Yes, the spring (or summer etc.) has ended

When did it end?

> It ended on ...

How long have you studied at this school?

> I've studied at this school for ...

285 When did you start your lessons at this school?

> I started my lessons at this school ... ago

Have you been to the cinema this year?

> Yes, I've been to the cinema this year ~ No, I haven't been to the cinema this year

When was the last time you went to the cinema?

> The last time I went to the cinema was ...

Have you written any dictations this week?

Yes, I've written some dictations this week ~ No, I haven't written any dictations this week

Did you write a dictation yesterday?

Yes, I wrote a dictation yesterday ~ No, I didn't write a dictation yesterday

wild

Are horses wild animals?

Some horses are wild animals

branch

What do we call the arms of a tree?

We call the arms of a tree "branches"

Does your bank have a branch near here?

Yes, my bank has a branch near here ~ No, my bank doesn't have a branch near here

bridge

Are there any bridges over the river in Paris?

Yes, there are some bridges over the river in Paris

egg

About how many eggs do you eat a week?

I eat about … eggs a week

push   pull

What am I doing?

You're pushing the table

What am I doing?

You're pulling the table

Do you push this door to go out of the classroom?

Yes, I push that door to go out of the classroom ~ No, I don't push that door to go out of the classroom; I pull it

Is this table too heavy for you to pull into the next room?

Yes, that table's too heavy for me to
pull into the next room ~ No, that table
isn't too heavy for me to pull into the next room

interest   bore

What subject interests you the most?

... interests
me the most

What subject bores you the most?

... bores me the most

287 ## interesting   interested   boring   bored

Do you think football's an interesting sport?

Yes, I think football's an
interesting sport ~ No, I don't think
football's an interesting sport; I think it's a boring sport

Are you interested in the history of your country?

Yes, I'm interested in
the history of my country ~ No, I'm
not interested in the history of my country

Do you get bored if you have nothing to do?

Yes, I get bored if I have
nothing to do ~ No, I don't
get bored if I have nothing to do

between   among   science

The difference between "between" and "among" is that we generally use "between" for two people or things, whereas we use "among" for more than two people or things. For example, "Between the two subjects of history and geography, I prefer geography", and "Among all the subjects I study (or studied) at school, I like (or liked) science the most".

What's the difference between "between" and "among"?

The difference between "between"
and "among" is that we generally use
"between" for two people or things, whereas we
use "among" for more than two people or things

Give me an example of each, please.

I'm sitting between the
teacher and the window.
I'm sitting among the other students.

Is there anybody sitting between you and me? Yes, there's somebody sitting between you and me ~ No, there isn't anybody sitting between you and me

288 **Among all the subjects you study (or studied) at school, which do (or did) you think is (or was) the most boring?** Among all the subjects I study (or studied) at school, I think (or thought) ... is (or was) the most boring

Among all the places you've ever been to, which do you think is the ugliest? Among all the places I've ever been to, I think ... is the ugliest

Among all the things in this room, are any yours? Yes, among all the things in this room, some are mine

 *Dictation 31*

The opposite of heaven is hell./ The poor dog is shaking with cold./ The public killed the queen./ Can you show me the way/ to the station, please?/ Our bodies contain a lot of blood./ Many teenagers don't like/ wearing a uniform for school./ Their glasses are full of water./ How do we form the past tense/ of regular verbs?/ We add the letters "ed"./ How often/ do you walk along/ this street?/ This way is the quickest./ I agree that smoking/ is bad for the health.

LESSON 56

289 <u>To be going to</u>

intention	soon	happen

One use of "to be going to" is to say what we think will happen because of something we know now. For example, "The sky is very dark now; I think it's going to rain", or "John is a very good student; he's going to do well in his exams".

Tell me one use of "to be going to".

One use of "to be going to" is to say what we think will happen because of something we know now

What am I going to do?

You're going to open the book; you're going to sit down, etc.

Do you think it's going to rain soon?

Yes, I think it's going to rain soon ~ No, I don't think it's going to rain soon

Another use of "to be going to" is to speak about our future intentions. For example, "I'm going to keep studying English for a few more years".

Tell me another use of "to be going to".

Another use of "to be going to" is to speak about our future intentions

What are you going to do after the lesson?

I'm going to go to work, go home, have lunch/dinner etc. after the lesson

290 Are you going to watch television this evening?

Yes, I'm going to watch television this evening ~ No, I'm not going to watch television this evening

What are you going to have for your dinner this evening?

I'm going to have ... for my dinner this evening

Are you going to come here again tomorrow?

Yes, I'm going to come here again tomorrow ~ No, I'm not going to come here again tomorrow; I'm going to come here again on ...

enjoy   museum

What kind of things do you enjoy doing most of all ?
The kind of things I enjoy doing most of all are watching television, going to the cinema etc.

Do you always enjoy your weekends?
Yes, I always enjoy my weekends ~ No, I don't always enjoy my weekends

Do you enjoy going to museums?
Yes, I enjoy going to museums ~ No, I don't enjoy going to museums

Do young children enjoy bedtime stories?
Yes, young children enjoy bedtime stories

hole   keyhole

What's this?
It's a hole

What kind of hole do we find in a door?
We find a keyhole in a door

291 Have you got a hole in your pocket (or pullover, socks etc.)?
Yes, I've got a hole in my pocket ~ No, I haven't got a hole in my pocket

stupid   intelligent   clever

Is it stupid to believe everything people tell you?
Yes, it's stupid to believe everything people tell you

Which do you think are more intelligent: cats or dogs?
I think ... are more intelligent than ...

What's another word for "intelligent"?
Another word for "intelligent" is "clever"

against

What am I doing?
You're pushing against the table

Who does this country play football against?
This country plays football against ...

Is the chair against the wall?
No, the chair isn't against the wall; it's near the wall

Is the chair against the wall now?
Yes, the chair's against the wall now

The past participle of the verb "to go" is "gone". The three forms of "go" are "go, went, gone".

292   What's the past participle of the verb "to go"?

> The past participle of the verb "to go" is "gone"

What are the three forms of "go"?

> The three forms of "go" are "go, went, gone"

We have two sentences:

1) "Mr Brown has been to Scotland" and

2) "Mr Brown has gone to Scotland".

The first sentence, "Mr Brown has been to Scotland", means that he has visited Scotland in his life but is not there now. The second sentence, "Mr Brown has gone to Scotland", means he is in Scotland; he isn't here now.

What's the difference between these two sentences?

"Mr Brown has been to Scotland"

and

"Mr Brown has gone to Scotland"

> The difference between those two sentences is that the first sentence means that Mr Brown has visited Scotland in his life but he is not there now, whereas the second sentence means he is in Scotland; he is not here now

We can say "Mr Brown has gone to Scotland", because he is not here now, but we can't say "I have gone to Scotland", because that means I am not here now, which is impossible.

Why can we say "Mr Brown has gone to Scotland", but not "I have gone to Scotland"?

> We can say "Mr Brown has gone to Scotland", but not "I have gone to Scotland", because "I have gone to Scotland" means I am not here now, which is impossible

Do you know anybody who keeps birds at home?

> Yes, I know somebody who keeps birds at home
> ~ No, I don't know anybody who keeps birds at home

When people go on holiday, do they generally prefer to fly or go by train?

> When people go on holiday
> they generally prefer to ...

Can a bird fly quicker than a plane (aeroplane)?

> No, a bird can't fly
> quicker than a plane; it flies
> slower than a plane (aeroplane)

Can a chicken fly?

> Yes, a chicken can fly, but not very far

Have you ever dreamt you could fly?

> Yes, I've sometimes dreamt I
> could fly ~ No, I've never dreamt I could fly

 *Dictation 32*

I had to meet him/ at the corner of the street,/ and he asked me/ to bring him some cash./ I cannot jump/ as high as the door./ The water we drink/ isn't completely pure;/ it's impure./ We can buy wine in supermarkets./ I never promise/ to do things/ and then not do them./ Adults are rarely/ as impolite as children./ Can I help you?/ They can express their thoughts/ quite well in English./ The past tenses of some irregular verbs/ are as follows:/ spoke, came, broke,/ wore, wrote, got up,/ stood, shone, took,/ told.

Do Revision Exercise 21

294 **fat** **thin**

What's the difference between "thick" and "fat"? The difference between "thick" and "fat" is that we use "thick" for things and "fat" for people and animals

Are you fatter than your mother? Yes, I'm fatter than my mother ~ No, I'm not fatter than my mother; I'm thinner than she is

Who's the thinnest person in your family? My ... is the thinnest person in my family

Do people generally become thinner as they become older? No, people don't generally become thinner as they become older; they become fatter

swam

What's the past of the verb "to swim"? The past of the verb "to swim" is "swam"

Did you swim last summer? Yes, I swam last summer ~ No, I didn't swim last summer

lost

What is the past simple and the past participle of the verb "to lose"? The past simple and the past participle of the verb "to lose" is "lost"

295 Have you ever lost your way in a large city? Yes, I've sometimes lost my way in a large city ~ No, I've never lost my way in a large city

Have you ever lost anything worth a lot of money? Yes, I've lost something worth a lot of money ~ No, I've never lost anything worth a lot of money

each other   one another

I am looking at you, and you are looking at me. We are looking at each other. I am looking at you, you are looking at me, I am looking at him, he is looking at me etc. We are looking at one another.

We generally use "each other" for two people or things, and "one another" for more than two people or things.

What's the difference between "each other" and "one another"?

> The difference between each other
> and one another is that we generally use
> "each other" for two people or things, and
> "one another" for more than two people or things

Give me an example, please.

> You and I are speaking
> to each other. The students
> speak to one another after the lesson

Do we look at each other during the lesson?

> Yes, we look at each
> other during the lesson

Do we shake hands with each other at the beginning of the lesson?

> Yes, we shake hands with each other at the
> beginning of the lesson ~ No, we don't shake
> hands with each other at the beginning of the lesson

296 Do your country and England play football against each other?

> Yes, my country and England play
> football against each other ~ No, my country
> and England don't play football against each other

Do Italy, Germany, Russia and England play football against one another?

> Yes, Italy, Germany, Russia and
> England play football against one another

Do the countries of Europe do business with one another?

> Yes, the countries of Europe
> do business with one another

Which language do the students speak to one another in after the lesson?

> The students speak to one
> another in ... after the lesson

to be able

am able – was able – been able

The past of "can" is "could", but "can" has no future tense. Therefore, we use the verb "to be able" and say "I will be able". The three forms of "to be able" are "am able, was able, been able".

What's the past of "can"?

The past of "can" is "could"

What's the future of "can"?

"Can" has no future.
Therefore, we use the verb
"to be able" and say "I will be able"

What's the infinitive of "can"?

"Can" has no infinitive.
Therefore, we use "to be able"

What are the three forms of "be able"?

The three forms of "be able"
are "am able, was able, been able"

297 Were you able to speak English a few years ago?

Yes, I was able to
speak English a few years ago ~ No, I
wasn't able to speak English a few years ago

Are you able to reach that book without standing up?

No, I'm not
able to reach that book without standing up

Will you be able to speak English well if you study a lot?

Yes, I'll be
able to speak English well if I study a lot

Have you been able to answer all the questions I have asked you without too much difficulty?

No, I haven't been
able to answer all the questions
you've asked me without too much
difficulty; some I have and some I haven't

factory

Tell me the names of some things that we make in factories

The names of some things that we
make in factories are cars, pens etc.

Do you think work in a factory can be pleasant?

Yes, I think
work in a factory can be pleasant
~ No, I don't think work in a factory can be pleasant

ordinary

Do soldiers wear ordinary clothes?

No, soldiers don't wear ordinary clothes; they wear uniforms

paint

Can you paint?

Yes, I can paint ~ No, I can't paint

298 **hotel**   **stay**

How much does it cost to stay in an ordinary hotel for one night in this town?

It costs about ... to stay in an ordinary hotel for one night in this town

 Dictation 33

In some countries/ people have to pay a tax/ if they have a dog./ The town was completely destroyed/ during the last war./ I'm sure he isn't guilty/ of the crime;/ he's too nice./ When we're hungry, we eat./ Fresh air is good for you./ Tell me first/ a geographical fact/ and then/ a historical fact, please./ He talked in a very low voice./ My birthday's in February./ Drove, saw, sat,/ ate, gave, began,/ drank, slept./ When he becomes a doctor,/ he'll get lots of money./ She doesn't like her new job.

LESSON 58

song

Can you understand all the words when you listen to a song in English?

> No, I can't understand all the
> words when I listen to a song in English

fun   **funny**

What's the difference between the words "fun" and "funny"?

> The difference between the words "fun"
> and "funny" is that if something is fun, we enjoy
> it, whereas if something is funny, it makes us laugh.

Do you sometimes go shopping with your friends at the weekend for fun?

> Yes, I sometimes go shopping with
> my friends at the weekend for fun ~ No, I
> never go shopping with my friends at the weekend for fun

What's the funniest film you've ever seen?

> ... is the funniest
> film I've ever seen

The three forms of some important verbs

have	– had	– had
am able	– was able	– been able
begin	– began	– begun
know	– knew	– known
swim	– swam	– swum
take	– took	– taken
shake	– shook	– shaken
write	– wrote	– written
forget	– forgot	– forgotten
break	– broke	– broken
eat	– ate	– eaten

Have you had your lunch today?   Yes, I've had my lunch today ~
                                              No, I haven't had my lunch today

Have you always been able to speak English as well as you speak it now?
                                              No, I haven't always been able
                                     to speak English as well as I speak it now

Has the spring (or summer, autumn or winter) begun?   No, the spring
                                     (or summer, autumn or winter) hasn't begun

Have you ever known anybody who could speak more than five
languages?   Yes, I've known somebody who could
                                  speak more than five languages ~ No, I've never
                              known anybody who could speak more than five languages

301 What's the furthest you've ever swum?   The furthest
                                                          I've ever swum is ...

simply

Is it possible to learn English simply by listening to English songs?
                                              No, it isn't possible to learn English
                                              simply by listening to English songs

by mistake

Have you ever taken things that weren't yours by mistake?
                                              Yes, I've sometimes taken things
                                     that weren't mine by mistake ~ No, I've
                                     never taken things that weren't mine by mistake

Have you shaken anybody's hand today?   Yes, I've shaken
                                              somebody's hand today ~ No,
                                     I haven't shaken anybody's hand today

Have you written anything this lesson?   Yes, I've written
                                              something this lesson ~ No,
                                     I haven't written anything this lesson

if   whether   doubt

The word "whether" means the same as "if". We usually use "whether"
when we have a doubt and say, for example, "I don't know whether it'll
rain tomorrow" or "Can you tell me whether he is in his office, please?" or
"I can't decide whether it's a good idea to go there".

What does the word "whether" mean and when do we generally use it?

The word "whether" means the same as "if" and we generally use it when we express a doubt

Give me an example, please.

I don't know whether he can speak English or not

Do you know whether I have any money in my pocket?

No, I don't know whether you have any money in your pocket

Do you have any idea whether they speak German or not?

No, I don't have any idea whether they speak German or not

Can you tell me whether it'll rain tomorrow or not?

No, I can't tell you whether it'll rain tomorrow or not

We also use "whether" when two possible actions have the same result. For example, if I go to France for my holiday, I will have a good time. Also, if I go to Spain for my holiday, I will have a good time. Therefore, I can say "Whether I go to France or Spain for my holiday, I will have a good time".

What's another use of the word "whether"?

Another use of the word "whether" is when two possible actions have the same result

Give me an example, please.

Whether it rains tomorrow or not, I'll go for a walk

What's the difference between these two sentences?

"I'm going to buy the car if it's cheap"

and

"I'm going to buy the car whether it's cheap or not"

The difference between these two sentences is that the first sentence means I'm going to buy the car only if it's cheap, whereas the second sentence means I'm going to buy the car if it's cheap or expensive; the price is not important.

speed

What is the highest speed a car can go when in town in this country?

The highest speed a car can go
when in town in this country is ...

surprise

Do you like unpleasant surprises?

No, I don't like
unpleasant surprises

Does it surprise you when somebody from another country speaks your language well?

Yes, it surprises me
when somebody from another
country speaks my language well

struggle

Is it a big struggle for you to get up on a cold winter's morning when you feel very tired?

Yes, it's a big struggle
for me to get up on a cold
winter's morning when I feel very tired

Do you sometimes struggle to understand people when they speak English quickly?

Yes, I sometimes
struggle to understand people
when they speak English quickly

 *Do Revision Exercise 22*

304 **surround**

What surrounds this building?

... surround/surrounds
this building

sword

When did soldiers stop using swords in battle?

Soldiers stopped
using swords in battle
more than a hundred years ago

computer　**internet**　**website**　**information**

Do you think computers make your life easier or more difficult?

I think computers make my life ...

Do you often use the internet for finding information?　Yes, I often use
the internet for finding information ~ No, I
don't often use the internet for finding information

Do you like shopping on the internet?

Yes, I like shopping
on the internet ~ No, I
don't like shopping on the internet

What are some of the most popular websites in the world?　Some of
the most popular websites in the world are ...

turn on　　　　**turn off**

What am I doing?　　　　You're turning the light on and off

305 Do you turn off your computer when you go to bed at night?

Yes, I turn off my computer when
I go to bed at night ~ No, I don't turn
off my computer when I go to bed at night

great   lake

The word '"great" generally means "very good" but it can sometimes mean "big" or "important". For example, "That film is great" means "That film is very good", but when we speak about "the Great Lakes" in North America, we mean that they are very big, and when we say that somebody is "a great man", we generally mean that they are important in public life.

What does the word "great" mean?

> The word "great" generally means "very good" but it can sometimes mean "big" or "important"

Give me an example of the word "great" meaning "very good".

> This film is great! I know a great restaurant near here

Who do you think is your greatest friend?

> I think my greatest friend is ...

Tell me the names of some great people in history.

> The names of some great people in history are Mahatma Gandhi, Albert Einstein, Marie Curie etc.

Who do you think was the greatest man that ever lived?

> I think ... was the greatest man that ever lived

Which is the greatest city in your country?

> is the greatest city in my country

306   kept   promise   keep a promise

break a promise

What is the past simple and the past participle of the verb "to keep"?

> The past simple and the past participle of the verb "to keep" is "kept"

Have you ever kept any animals at home?

> Yes, I've kept some animals at home ~ No, I've never kept any animals at home

What's the opposite of "to keep a promise"?

> The opposite of "to keep a promise" is "to break a promise"

Have you always kept your promises?

Yes, I've always kept my promises ~ No, I haven't always kept my promises; sometimes I've broken them

found

What's the past simple and the past participle of "find"?

The past simple and the past participle of "find" is "found"

Did you find English very difficult when you began studying it?

Yes, I found English very difficult when I began studying it

Have you ever found anything on the street worth a lot of money?

Yes, I've found something on the street worth a lot of money ~ No, I've never found anything on the street worth a lot of money

else

What else do people do in the evening besides watching TV?

People eat, read, go for walks etc. in the evening besides watching TV

Do you study anything else besides English?

Yes, I study something else besides English ~ No, I don't study anything else besides English

What else do you study?

I also study ... ~ I study nothing else

Does anybody else in your family speak English besides you?

Yes, somebody else in my family speaks English besides me ~ No, nobody else in my family speaks English besides me

fast

"Fast" means the same as "quick" or "quickly"; it is both an adjective and an adverb. We do not add "ly" to it. We say "He writes fast", and not "He writes fastly".

What does the word "fast" mean?

The word "fast" means the same as "quick" or "quickly"

Are you a fast writer?

Yes, I'm a fast writer ~ No, I'm not a fast writer

Do you walk fast when the weather is very hot?

No, I don't walk fast
when the weather is very hot; I walk slowly

308   music   dance   rhythm

sense of rhythm

Do you go dancing very much?

Yes, I go dancing a lot
~ No, I don't go dancing very much

Is it easier to dance well if you have a good sense of rhythm?

Yes, it's easier to dance well
if you have a good sense of rhythm

Do you prefer dancing to fast or slow music?

I prefer
dancing to ... music

just   done

The word "just" can mean "a short time ago" and it can also mean "simply" or "only".

What are the three forms of "do"?

The three forms
of "do" are "do, did, done"

What does the word "just" mean?

The word "just"
can mean "a short time ago"
and it can also mean "simply" or "only"

What have I just done?

You've just closed your book

Have you just come into the room?

Yes, I've just
come into the room ~ No, I
haven't just come into the room

When somebody makes you angry, do you say something or do you just stay quiet?

When somebody
makes me angry, I ...

309 Are there many shops in the place where you live or just a few?

There are ... shops in the place where I live

real

Have you ever seen a real tiger?

Yes, I've seen a real tiger
~ No, I've never seen a real tiger

Is James Bond a real person?

No, James Bond isn't a real person

 *Dictation 34*

That artist painted/ many pictures of bridges./ I must reach the shop/ before it closes/ because I want to buy some chicken/ for lunch tomorrow./ He feels much stronger today;/ yesterday he was very weak./ Some people/ are willing to die/ for what they believe./ Are you sure/ the desk is in the middle?/ Last night/ I had a very bad dream./ It is a crime/ to refuse a poor man money./ Their garden is separate from ours./ Left, smelt, learnt,/ sent, knew, hung,/ read, met./ I made eight mistakes last time.

LESSON 60

probable   **improbable**   **probably**

Is it probable that it will snow next summer?

No, it isn't probable that it will snow next summer; it's very improbable

Are you probably going to finish all of the stages of the Callan Method?

Yes, I'm probably going to finish all of the stages of the Callan Method ~ No, I'm probably not going to finish all of the stages of the Callan Method

 *See Chart 8*

possibility   **imagine**   **construction**

police   **police station**   **park**

1st Conditional

"If" + present + "will do" = real possibility

If I go to the park tomorrow, I will play football

This sentence means that I think there is a <u>real possibility</u> that I will go to the park tomorrow, and, if I do, I will play football. The construction of the 1st conditional is "If" + present + "will do". It communicates that we think something is a real possibility.

2nd Conditional

"If + past + "would do" = only imagining

If I went to the park tomorrow, I would play football

This sentence means that I think it is <u>very improbable</u> that I will go to the park tomorrow; I am <u>only imagining</u> it. The construction of the 2nd conditional is "If" + past + "would do". It communicates that we are only imagining something.

It is important to understand that, in the 2nd conditional, we use the past simple after "if", but we are not thinking about past time; we are thinking about now, the future or general time. For example:

If I had £1 million (now), I would buy a house

If we went to the cinema tomorrow (future), we would see a film

If they were American (general time), they would speak English

When do we use the 1st conditional?

> We use the 1st conditional to communicate that we think something is a real possibility

Give me an example, please.

> If he sees his friend, he will say "hello"

When do we use the 2nd conditional?

> We use the 2nd conditional to communicate that we are only imagining something

Give me an example, please.

> If she went to the North Pole, she would feel very cold. If they were stronger, they would be able to lift the table

If you feel tired tonight, will you go to bed early?

> Yes, if I feel tired tonight, I will go to bed early

If you felt ill tomorrow, would you go out?

> No, if I felt ill tomorrow, I wouldn't go out; I would stay at home

If you study hard, will you learn to speak English well?

> Yes, if I study hard, I will learn to speak English well

If you stopped studying, would your English get better?

No, if I stopped studying, my English wouldn't get better; it would get worse

If you had £1 million, what would you buy?

If I had £1 million, I would buy ...

If you came here next Sunday, would you be able to have a lesson?

No, if I came here next Sunday, I wouldn't be able to have a lesson

Why not?

Because the school is closed on Sundays

If you swam in the sea in the middle of winter, would you find the water warm?

No, if I swam in the sea in the middle of winter, I wouldn't find the water warm; I would find it cold

If you go on holiday next year, where will you go?

If I go on holiday next year, I will go to ...

If you found something in the street worth a lot of money, would you keep it or would you take it to the police station?

If I found something in the street worth a lot of money, I would keep it/take it to the police station

If you sent a letter and forgot to put the address on it, would it arrive?

No, if I sent a letter and forgot to put the address on it, it wouldn't arrive

313 *Dictation 35*

I'll listen to the news/ on a different radio station today./ When I feel ill, I go to bed./ When I feel thirsty,/ my favourite drink is water./ The difference between a ship and a boat/ is that a boat is small/ whereas a ship is large./ I want a credit card/ from a bank with a branch/ in every town/ in the country./ Most horses are not wild./ The river is very shallow,/ but we can go over by bridge/ if you like./ I generally have two eggs for breakfast.

 *Do Revision Exercise 23*

Grammar questions

1) When do we use "a" before a word, and when do we use "an"? Give me an example of each.

We use "a" before a word beginning with a consonant sound, and "an" before a word beginning with a vowel sound. For example, a book; an ashtray.

2) When does the pronunciation of the word "the" change? Give me an example.

The pronunciation of the word "the" changes before a word beginning with a vowel. For example, the /ðə/ book; the /ðiː/ ashtray.

3) What's the difference between "any" and "some"? Give me an example of each.

The difference between "any" and "some" is that we use "any" in questions and negative sentences, whereas we use "some" in positive sentences. For example, "Are there any books on the table?" – "Yes, there are some books on the table", and "Are there any books on the floor?" – "No, there aren't any books on the floor".

4) What's the difference between the present continuous and the present simple?

The difference between the present continuous and the present simple is that we use the present continuous for an action we are doing now, whereas we use the present simple for an action we do generally. For example, "I'm speaking English now but I generally speak French".

5) Where does the preposition generally come in an English sentence with a question word? Give me an example.

The preposition generally comes last in an English sentence with a question word. For example, "Who are you speaking to?"

6) What's the difference between "into" and "in"? Give me an example of each.

The difference between "into" and "in" is that we use "into" for a thing that moves from one place to another, and "in" for a thing that remains in one place. For example, "I'm putting my hand into my pocket. My hand is in my pocket".

7) **What's the difference between a possessive adjective and a possessive pronoun? Give me an example of each.** The difference between a possessive adjective and a possessive pronoun is that we put a possessive adjective in front of a noun, whereas we use a possessive pronoun instead of a noun. For example, "This is my book. This book is mine".

8) **What are the possessive adjectives?** The possessive adjectives are "my", "your", "his", "her", "its", "our", "your", "their".

9) **What are the possessive pronouns?** The possessive pronouns are "mine", "yours", "his", "hers", "ours", "yours", "theirs".

10) **When do we use "many" and "few" and when do we use "much" and "little"? Give me an example of each.** We use "many" and "few" for things we can count, whereas we use "much" and "little" for things we can't count. For example, "many books", "much water", "few pens", "little wine".

11) **Why do we say "cheaper than" but not "expensiver than"?** We say "cheaper than", but not "expensiver than", because the adjective "cheap" has only one syllable, whereas the adjective "expensive" has three syllables.

12) **Do we use the gerund or the infinitive after a preposition? Give me an example.** We use the gerund after a preposition. For example, "before coming; after taking; for buying etc."

13) **What is a gerund?** A gerund is a noun that we make by putting the letters 'ing' at the end of a verb.

14) **What's the difference between "to look at" and "to watch"?** The difference between "to look at" and "to watch" is that we use "to look at" for something that is still, whereas we use "to watch" for something that is moving.

15) **What's the difference between "ever" and "never"?** The difference between "ever" and "never" is that the word "ever" is positive, and we generally use it in questions, whilst the word "never" is negative.

16) **What's the difference between "quick" and "quickly"? Give me an example of each.**

The difference between "quick" and "quickly" is that "quick" is an adjective, whereas "quickly" is an adverb. For example, "He is a quick writer; he writes quickly".

17) **What's the difference between "over" and "on"?**

The difference between "over" and "on" is that we say "over" when there is no contact between the two objects, or when one object covers the other completely, whereas we use "on" when there is contact and when one object doesn't cover the other completely.

18) **How do we form the past tense of regular verbs?**

We form the past tense of regular verbs by putting the letters "ed" at the end. For example, "walk – walked".

19) **What's the difference between "bring" and "take"?**

The difference between "bring" and "take" is that "bring" means "carry here" whereas "take" means "carry there". For example, "Bring your book here, please. Take your book home".

20) **When do we use "shall" instead of "will"?**

We use "shall" instead of "will" when we are making a suggestion with the pronoun "I" or "we".

21) **What are the common ways of asking a question with the verb "to have"?**

The common ways of asking a question with the verb "to have" are "Do you have a pen?" and "Have you got a pen?"

22) **What do we usually put after the verb "succeed"? Give me an example.**

We usually put the word "in" and a gerund after the verb "succeed". For example, "She always succeeds in getting what she wants".

23) **What's the difference between "I don't have to do it" and "I mustn't do it"?**

The difference between "I don't have to do it" and "I mustn't do it" is that "I don't have to do it" means that I can do it if I want but it is not necessary, whereas "I mustn't do it" means that it is bad or wrong to do it.

24) **What's the difference between the present perfect and the past simple? Give me an example of each.** The difference between the present perfect and the past simple is that we use the present perfect when we are thinking about time before or up to now, whereas we use the past simple when we are thinking about a specific past time. For example, "I have been here for twenty minutes; I arrived here twenty minutes ago".

25) **Why don't we usually say "littler" and "littlest"?** We don't usually say "littler" and "littlest" because they're difficult to pronounce. Instead, we use "smaller" and "smallest".

26) **What are the three forms of an English verb? Give me an example.** The three forms of an English verb are the present, the past and the past participle. For example, "see, saw, seen".

27) **What do we sometimes mean when we use the words "one", "you", "we" and "they"?** When we use the words "one", "you", "we" and "they", we sometimes mean people in general.

28) **Which do we generally use the most: "one", "you" or "we"?** We generally use "you" the most.

29) **What are the three ways in which we can use the present perfect? Give me an example of each.** The three ways in which we can use the present perfect are when we talk about our experiences, when we talk about the duration of an action up to now, and when we talk about the result now of a past action.For example, "I've read that book; I've studied English for two years; I've cut my finger".

30) **What's the difference between "between" and "among"?** The difference between "between" and "among" is that we generally use "between" for two people or things, whereas we use "among" for more than two people or things.

31) **When do we use "to be going to"?** We use "to be going to" to say what we think will happen because of something we know now, and to speak about our future intentions. For example, "I think it's going to rain soon", and "I'm going to buy a new car".

32) What are the three forms of the verbs "to be" and "to go"?

The three forms of the verbs
"to be" and "to go" are "am,
was, been" and "go, went, gone".

33) Why can I say "Mr Brown has gone to Scotland", but not "I have gone to Scotland"?

Because "I have gone to Scotland"
means I am not here now, which is impossible.

34) What's the difference between "each other" and "one another"?

The difference between "each other"
and "one another" is that we generally
use "each other" for two people or things and
"one another" for more than two people or things.

35) What are the past, future and infinitive of "can"?

The past of "can" is "could" or
"was able"; it has no future or infinitive, so we use
"will be able" for the future, and "to be able" for the infinitive.

36) When do we use the 1st conditional? Give me an example.

We use the 1st conditional to communicate
that we think something is a real possibility. For
example, "If it rains again tomorrow, I will take an umbrella".

37) When do we use the 2nd conditional? Give me an example.

We use the 2nd conditional to communicate
that we are only imagining something. For example,
"If she had a better job, she would earn more money".

Irregular verbs

present	past	past participle
am	was	been
become	became	become
begin	began	begun
break	broke	broken
bring	brought	brought
build	built	built
buy	bought	bought
come	came	come
cost	cost	cost
cut	cut	cut
do	did	done
dream	dreamt	dreamt
drink	drank	drunk
eat	ate	eaten
feel	felt	felt
find	found	found
fly	flew	flown
forget	forgot	forgotten
get	got	got
give	gave	given
go	went	gone
hang	hung	hung
have	had	had
hold	held	held
keep	kept	kept
know	knew	known
learn	learnt	learnt
leave	left	left
mean	meant	meant

meet	met	met
mistake	mistook	mistaken
put	put	put
say	said	said
see	saw	seen
sell	sold	sold
send	sent	sent
shake	shook	shaken
shine	shone	shone
show	showed	shown
sit	sat	sat
sleep	slept	slept
smell	smelt	smelt
speak	spoke	spoken
stand	stood	stood
take	took	taken
teach	taught	taught
tell	told	told
think	thought	thought
wear	wore	worn

List of tenses

Imperative
Eat! – Don't eat!

Present continuous
I am eating – I am not eating – Am I eating?

Present simple
I eat – I do not eat – Do I eat?

Infinitive with "to"
To eat – I want to eat

Infinitive without "to"
eat – I must eat

Gerund
eating – I like eating

Past simple
I ate – I did not eat – Did I eat?

Future
I will eat – I will not eat – Will I eat?

Present perfect
I have eaten – I have not eaten – Have I eaten?

Future intention
I am going to eat – I am not going to eat – Am I going to eat?

1st conditional
If I eat good food, I will stay healthy

2nd conditional
If I ate too much, I would feel bad

Revision Exercise 14 (Lessons 32 – 33)

1   Have you got as much money as a millionaire?

2   Is it very cold in Africa?

3   What message do we generally write inside a Christmas card?

4   Do you feel sad when you go on holiday?

5   What do you eat for your lunch apart from meat?

6   Do you speak English better than your language?

7   When do we use capital letters?

8   Where do you think's the best place in this country to live?

9   Name me some games in which we use a ball.

10 What's the difference between "to look at" and "to watch"?

11 Where do you buy your food?

12 Do we use the gerund or the infinitive after a preposition?

13 Give me some examples, please.

14 What is a gerund?

15 What do you do before coming to school each day?

16 What's the difference between "beside" and "besides"?

17 Is Paris beside the sea?

18 What do you do in the evening besides watching television?

19 Have you got another watch besides that one?

20 Do most people in this country go to church (or temple, synagogue or mosque) each week?

Answers

1   No, I haven't got as much money as a millionaire; I've got less money than a millionaire.

2   No, it isn't very cold in Africa; it's very hot in Africa.

3   The message we generally write inside a Christmas card is "A Merry Christmas and a Happy New Year".

4   No, I don't feel sad when I go on holiday; I feel happy.

5   I eat bread, vegetables etc. for my lunch apart from meat.

6   No, I don't speak English better than my language; I speak it worse than my language.

7   We use capital letters at the beginning of a sentence, for the pronoun "I", and for the first letter of people's names, place names, days of the week, months of the year, nationalities and languages.

8   I think ...is the best place in this country to live.

9   Some games in which we use a ball are football, tennis, rugby, golf, basketball etc.

10   The difference between "to look at" and "to watch" is that we use "to look at" for something that is still, whilst we use "to watch" for something that is moving.

11   I buy my food from a shop near where I live.

12   We use the gerund after a preposition.

13   before coming; after taking; for buying etc.

14   A gerund is a noun that we make by putting the letters 'ing' at the end of a verb.

15   I eat breakfast, speak to my friends etc. before coming to school each day.

16   The difference between "beside" and "besides" is that "beside" means "next to" whereas "besides" means "apart from".

17   No, Paris isn't beside the sea; it's inland.

18   I go for a walk, I read, I go to the cinema etc. in the evening besides watching television.

19   Yes, I've got another watch besides this one. ~ No, I haven't got another watch besides this one.

20   Yes, most people in this country go to church (temple, synagogue or mosque) each week. ~ No, most people in this country don't go to church (or temple, synagogue or mosque) each week.

Revision Exercise 15 (Lessons 34 – 35)

1   What covers our heads?

2   Does it generally snow very much in the hot countries of the world?

3   Can you hold a complicated conversation in English?

4   Do you know any excellent restaurants near here?

5   Do people walk quicker in hot weather than in cold?

6   Do we say "every student is good" or "every students are good"? Why?

7   When it rains what do we cover our heads with?

8   Do you always reply to letters you receive?

9   Is the weather nicer today than yesterday?

10   Are you always nice to other people?

11   Where were you at this time yesterday?

12   What's the difference between a road and a street?

13   Are there a lot of lines on an old person's face?

14   After drinking a bottle of whisky, can people walk in a straight line?

15   Do you always get up at the same time every morning?

16   Can you text as quickly as you can speak?

17   Is the River Thames deeper than the Mediterranean Sea?

18   Do people study subjects deeply at university?

19   When people smoke, where do they put the ash?

20   Is it pleasant to wait for somebody in the rain?

Answers

1   Our hair covers our heads.

2   No, it doesn't generally snow very much in the hot countries of the world; it generally snows very little.

3   No, I can't hold a complicated conversation in English; I can hold a simple conversation in English

4   Yes, I know some excellent restaurants near here. ~ No, I don't know any excellent restaurants near here.

5   No, people don't walk quicker in hot weather than in cold; they walk slower.

6   We say every student is good; because "every" is singular.

7   When it rains we cover our heads with a hat or an umbrella.

8   Yes, I always reply to letters I receive. ~ No, I don't always reply to letters I receive.

9   Yes, the weather's nicer today than yesterday. ~ No, the weather isn't nicer today than yesterday; it's worse.

10   Yes, I'm always nice to other people. ~ No, I'm not always nice to other people.

11   I was ... at this time yesterday.

12   The difference between a road and a street is that a road is generally in the country and connects two towns, whereas a street is in a town and generally has shops in it.

13 Yes, there are a lot of lines on an old person's face.

14 No, after drinking a bottle of whisky, people can't walk in a straight line; they walk in a crooked line.

15 No, I don't always get up at the same time every morning; sometimes I get up early and sometimes I get up late.

16 No, I can't text as quickly as I can speak; I text more slowly than I speak

17 No, the River Thames isn't deeper than the Mediterranean Sea; it's shallower than the Mediterranean Sea.

18 Yes, people study subjects deeply at university.

19 When people smoke, they put the ash in an ashtray.

20 No, it isn't pleasant to wait for somebody in the rain; it's unpleasant.

Revision Exercise 16 (Lessons 36 – 37)

1 What's the difference between the words "ever" and "never"?

2 Is Christmas ever on the 21st of December?

3 Is the face of your watch square?

4 Do we nod our heads when we say "no"?

5 What do we call this direct method we are using for learning English?

6 By this method does the student translate before speaking?

7 Are the countries of Europe more or less friends today?

8 What kind of accent do you speak English with?

9 During the day it's light, whilst during the night it's dark. What does this depend on?

10 What are clouds made of?

11 Do you always remember everything you learn?

12 Is it nearly time to go to bed?

13 Were you here a hundred years ago?

14 Are there any fields near where you live?

15 Is the number of people in your town always increasing?

16 Were there a lot of battles in Europe during the Second World War?

17 What's over this building?

18 Does the sun often shine in the north of Europe in winter?

19 Do you understand two people when they speak very quickly in English?

20 Do you think it's easy to stop smoking?

Answers

1   The difference between the words "ever" and "never" is that the word "ever" is positive, and is generally used in questions, whilst the word "never" is negative.

2   No, Christmas is never on the 21st of December; it's always on the 25th of December.

3   No, the face of my watch isn't square; it's round.

4   No, we don't nod our heads when we say "no"; we shake our heads when we say "no".

5   We call this direct method we are using for learning English the Callan Method.

6   No, by this method the student doesn't translate before speaking; he thinks and speaks directly in the new language.

7   Yes, the countries of Europe are more or less friends today.

8   I speak English with a/an ... accent.

9   It depends on the sun and where it is in the sky.

10 Clouds are made of water.

11 No, I don't always remember everything I learn; some things I remember and some things I forget.

12 Yes, it's nearly time to go to bed. ~ No, it isn't nearly time to go to bed.

13 No, I wasn't here a hundred years ago.

14 Yes, there are some fields near where I live. ~ No, there aren't any fields near where I live.

15 Yes, the number of people in my town is always increasing.

16 Yes, there were a lot of battles in Europe during the Second World War.

17 The sky's over this building.

18 No, the sun doesn't often shine in the north of Europe in winter; it rarely shines.

19 No, I don't understand two people when they speak very quickly in English.

20 Yes, I think it's easy to stop smoking. ~ No, I don't think it's easy to stop smoking.

Revision Exercise 17 (Lesson 38 – 39)

1   Do you talk to your friends on your mobile every day?

2   Is it right to say "I am talking English"?

3   Did you watch television last week?

4   Did you talk to anybody in your family last week?

5   Did you want to come to school today?

6   Can you see any trees from where you're sitting?

7   Name some animals we can see on a farm.

8   Can we measure exactly the quantity of water in the sea?

9   Is it necessary to study a lot if we want to learn a subject well?

10 When you have a meal in a restaurant, do you generally pay by cash or by (credit) card?

11 Which streets do you walk along when you go home?

12 What's the best way to learn a language?

13 How often do you go to the cinema?

14 Which is healthier to have with our lunch: chips or salad?

15 Do you always agree with everything people say?

16 What do we sometimes add to our tea and coffee?

17 Can you jump as high as a house?

18 Can you sit at the corner of a round table?

19 Does almost everybody in this country have a mobile phone?

20 In some jobs, can people work from home instead of going to an office?

Answers

1   Yes, I talk to my friends on my mobile every day. ~No, I don't talk to my friends on my mobile every day.

2   No, it isn't right to say "I am talking English"; it's wrong.

3   Yes, I watched television last week.

4   Yes, I talked to somebody in my family last week. ~ No, I didn't talk to anybody in my family last week.

5   Yes, I wanted to come to school today. ~ No, I didn't want to come to school today.

6   Yes, I can see some trees from where I'm sitting. ~ No, I can't see any trees from where I'm sitting.

7   On a farm, we can see pigs, cows, sheep, chickens and horses.

8   No, we can't measure exactly the quantity of water in the sea.

9   Yes, it's necessary to study a lot if we want to learn a subject well.

10   When I have a meal in a restaurant, I generally pay by ...

11   I walk along ... when I go home.

12   The best way to learn a language is to study a lot and repeat, repeat and repeat.

13   I go to the cinema about once a ...

14   Salad is healthier to have with our lunch than chips.

15   No, I don't always agree with everything people say; sometimes I agree and sometimes I disagree.

16   We sometimes add milk and sugar to our tea and coffee.

17   No, I can't jump as high as a house.

18   No, I can't sit at the corner of a round table.

19   Yes, almost everybody in this country has a mobile phone.

20   Yes, in some jobs, people can work from home instead of going to an office.

Revision Exercise 18 (Lesson 40 – 41)

1   What do we say to people on their birthday?

2   What can we do when we meet somebody for the first time?

3   What's the difference between "bring" and "take"?

4   Do you take a camera with you when you go on holiday?

5   Do you go to the cinema quite often?

6   Do you think learning English is quite easy, quite difficult, or very difficult?

7   Is pure water bad for the body?

8   Do you always do what you promise to do?

9   Are waiters and waitresses always polite to people in restaurants?

10   When we want to speak to somebody we don't know, what's the first thing we generally say?

11   Do husbands in this country generally help their wives in the house?

12   Which is the broadest street in your town?

13   Name me one of the poorest countries in the world?

14   Do parents in your country read bedtime stories to their children?

15   Can you express a very simple idea quite well in English?

16   Did you ever break an arm or a leg when you were a little child?

17   What time did you get up this morning?

18   Did you take any photographs on your last holiday?

19   What did you eat for your lunch yesterday?

20   How long did you sleep last night?

Answers

1   We say "Happy Birthday" to people on their birthday.

2   When we meet somebody for the first time, we can say "Hello. Nice to meet you", and shake hands with them.

3   The difference between "bring" and "take" is that "bring" means "carry here" whereas "take" means "carry there".

4   Yes, I take a camera with me when I go on holiday. ~ No, I don't take a camera with me when I go on holiday.

5   Yes, I go to the cinema quite often. ~ No, I don't go to the cinema very often.

6   I think learning English is …

7   No, pure water isn't bad for the body; it's good for the body.

8   Yes, I always do what I promise to do ~ No, I don't always do what I promise to do

9   No, waiters and waitresses aren't always polite to people in restaurants; sometimes they're polite and sometimes they're impolite.

10   When we want to speak to somebody we don't know, the first thing we generally say is "Excuse me".

11   Yes, husbands in this country generally help their wives in the house. ~ No, husbands in this country don't generally help their wives in the house.

12   … is the broadest street in my town.

13   … is one of the poorest countries in the world.

14   Yes, parents in my country read bedtime stories to their children. ~ No, parents in my country don't read bedtime stories to their children.

15   Yes, I can express a very simple idea quite well in English.

16 Yes, I broke an arm/a leg when I was a little child. ~ No, I never broke an arm or a leg when I was a little child.

17 I got up at ... this morning.

18 Yes, I took some photographs on my last holiday. ~ No, I didn't take any photographs on my last holiday.

19 I ate some ... for my lunch yesterday.

20 I slept ... hours last night.

Revision Exercise 19 (Lessons 42 – 43)

1 Are there any hills around this town/city?

2 Were Britain and America enemies during the Second World War?

3 Are you hungry at the moment?

4 Are there a lot of hungry people in some parts of the world today?

5 Do you think your English is getting better?

6 When you get hungry, what do you do?

7 Do you get (receive) any cards from your friends on your birthday?

8 When children are young, do their parents get (fetch) them from school each day?

9 What are the general meanings of the verb "get"?

10 Do most people die before they're a hundred years old?

11 Are young boys generally physically stronger than men?

12 What do we call the clothes that a soldier wears?

13 Which country do you think has the largest army in the world today?

14 Was Picasso a writer or an artist?

15 Do you always feel in good health?

16 Do people drive their cars in the middle of the road?

17 What's another word for "middle"?

18 Do we say "please" in English at the beginning of a request?

19 Are you Mr Brown or Mr Smith?

20 Are you always willing to help other people?

Answers

1 Yes, there are some hills around this town/city. ~ No, there aren't any hills around this town/city.

2 No, Britain and America weren't enemies during the Second World War; they were friends.

3 Yes, I'm hungry at the moment. ~ No, I'm not hungry at the moment.

4 Yes, there are a lot of hungry people in some parts of the world today.

5 Yes, I think my English is getting better.

6 When I get hungry, I eat.

7 Yes, I get some cards from my friends on my birthday. ~ No, I don't get any cards from my friends on my birthday.

8 Yes, when children are young, their parents get them from school each day.

9 The general meanings of the verb "get" are "become" and "obtain".

10 Yes, most people die before they are a hundred years old.

11 No, young boys aren't generally physically stronger than men; they're generally physically weaker than men.

12 We call the clothes that a soldier wears a uniform.

13 I think ... has the largest army in the world today.

14 Picasso was an artist.

15 Yes, I always feel in good health. ~ No, I don't always feel in good health.

16 No, people don't drive their cars in the middle of the road; in most countries they drive them on the right-hand side of the road.

17 Another word for "middle" is "centre".

18 No, we don't say please in English at the beginning of a request; we say it at the end of a request.

19 No, I'm neither Mr Brown nor Mr Smith; I'm ...

20 Yes, I'm always willing to help other people. ~ No, I'm not always willing to help other people.

Revision Exercise 20 (Lessons 44 – 45)

1 What time did you leave home to come here today?

2 Did you learn any new words last week?

3 Did you send any emails to your friends last month?

4   Did you feel cold last summer?

5   Where did you buy your clothes from?

6   Did you go to the pub last month?

7   Did you think the last film you saw was a good one?

8   Did your parents teach you to wash and dress when you were a child?

9   Did you hear the news on the radio yesterday?

10 Do you take medicine when you feel ill?

11 What's your favourite drink apart from water when you feel very thirsty?

12 Do they sell food in clothes shops?

13 If you have lots of work to do and a friend talks to you all the time, what do you tell him to do?

14 Does this country do business with foreign countries?

15 What is the price of a meal in a very cheap restaurant in the place where you live?

16 Is a bush higher (or taller) than a tree?

17 Is your watch worth as much now as it was when you bought it?

18 Do you think it is worth buying an umbrella if you live in a country where it only rains about once a month?

19 Is English grammar hard?

20 Is the floor soft?

Answers

1   I left home at ... to come here today.

2   Yes, I learnt some new words last week.

3   Yes, I sent some emails to my friends last month.

4   No, I didn't feel cold last summer; I felt hot.

5   I bought my clothes from ... (or "a clothes shop").

6   Yes, I went to the pub last month. ~ No, I didn't go to the pub last month.

7   Yes, I thought the last film I saw was a good one. ~ No, I didn't think the last film I saw was a good one; I thought it was bad.

8   Yes, my parents taught me to wash and dress when I was a child.

9   Yes, I heard the news on the radio yesterday. ~ No, I didn't hear the news on the radio yesterday.

10 Yes, I take medicine when I feel ill. ~ No, I don't take medicine when I feel ill.

11 My favourite drink apart from water when I feel very thirsty is ...

12 No, they don't sell food in clothes shops; they sell it in supermarkets.

13 If I have lots of work to do and a friend talks to me all the time, I tell him to go away.

14 Yes, this country does business with foreign countries.

15 The price of a meal in a very cheap restaurant in the place where I live is about ...

16 No, a bush isn't higher (or taller) than a tree; it's lower (shorter) than a tree.

17 No, my watch isn't worth as much now as it was when I bought it; it's worth less now than it was when I bought it.

18 No, I don't think it's worth buying an umbrella if I live in a country where it only rains about once a month.

19 No, English grammar isn't hard; it's easy.

20 No, the floor isn't soft; it's hard.

Revision Exercise 21 (Lessons 46 – 47)

1   What's the complete future of the verb "to go"?

2   What's the contraction of "I will"?

3   What's the opposite of 3 months ago?

4   Will it rain next year?

5   What's the contraction of "I will not"?

6   Will you be here in 100 years' time?

7   When do we use "shall" instead of "will"?

8   Can we use "shall" to ask for a suggestion?

9   Is this building open to the public?

10 Do you like speaking in public?

11 Do tigers kill other animals for food?

12 Are there many countries in the world which have a queen as the head of the government?

13 What colour's blood?

14 When you're eating chocolates in company, do you offer them round?

15 Do you think life is harder these days than it was in the past?

16 In your country, what colour do you use for death?

17 What do doctors suggest doing for a healthy life?

18 What will you do before going to bed tonight?

19 What do you do when you feel tired?

20 If you turn round, what will you see?

Answers

1 The complete future of the verb "to go" is "I will go", "You will go" etc.

2 The contraction of "I will" is "I'll".

3 The opposite of "3 months ago" is "in 3 months' time".

4 Yes, it'll rain next year.

5 The contraction of "I will not" is "I won't".

6 No, I won't be here in 100 years' time.

7 We use "shall" when we are making a suggestion with the pronoun "I" or "we".

8 Yes, we can use "shall" to ask for a suggestion.

9 No, this building isn't open to the public.

10 Yes, I like speaking in public. ~ No, I don't like speaking in public.

11 Yes, tigers kill other animals for food.

12 No, there aren't many countries in the world which have a queen as the head of the government.

13 Blood's red.

14 Yes, when I'm eating chocolates in company, I offer them round. ~ No, when I'm eating chocolates in company, I don't offer them round.

15 No, I don't think life is harder these days than it was in the past; I think it's easier.

16 In my country, we use ... for death.

17 Doctors suggest eating healthy food and getting lots of fresh air and exercise for a healthy life.

18 I'll watch TV, read, or go to the cinema etc. before going to bed tonight.

19 When I feel tired, I go to bed.

20 If I turn round, I'll see a picture etc.

Revision Exercise 22 (Lesson 48 – 49)

1   Do you often read magazines?

2   In a restaurant, what do we look at to decide what we want to eat?

3   Did you decide to study English, or did somebody in your family decide for you?

4   Explain the difference between the present continuous and the present simple, please.

5   Is it a good idea to book a table before going to a very popular restaurant?

6   Are you always willing to try anything new?

7   Are motorbikes quieter than bicycles?

8   What did you have for your breakfast this morning?

9   Could you read when you were a little baby?

10   Do you think maybe you'll go to the cinema next month?

11   Do you think it's easier to understand written English or spoken English?

12   Will the door be the same colour next week as it is this week?

13   Do you prefer to communicate with your friends by phoning or texting?

14   What are the common ways of asking a question with the verb "to have"?

15   What are the common ways for the past tense?

16   Which is the most common way of asking a question with the verb 'have' in the past?

17   Did you have your book with you last lesson?

18   Is it easier to become good at a sport if you get lots of practice?

19   What can we say when we offer something to somebody?

20   Would you like to visit Australia in the future?

Answers

1   Yes, I often read magazines. ~ No, I don't often read magazines.

2   In a restaurant, we look at a menu to decide what we want to eat.

3   I decided to study English; nobody in my family decided for me. ~ Somebody in my family decided for me.

4   The difference between the present continuous and the present simple is that we use the present continuous for an action we are doing now, whereas we use the present simple for an action we do generally.

5   Yes, it's a good idea to book a table before going to a very popular restaurant.

6   Yes, I'm always willing to try anything new. ~ No, I'm not always willing to try anything new.

7   No, motorbikes aren't quieter than bicycles; they're noisier than bicycles.

8   I had some coffee, some bread etc. for my breakfast this morning.

9   No, I couldn't read when I was a little baby.

10 Yes, I think maybe I'll go to the cinema next month. ~ No, I don't think I'll go to the cinema next month.

11 I think it's easier to understand ... English.

12 Yes, the door'll be the same colour next week as it is this week.

13 I prefer to communicate with my friends by ...

14 The common ways of asking a question with the verb "to have" are 1) Do you have a pen? and 2) Have you got a pen?

15 The common ways for the past tense are 1) Did you have a pen? 2) Had you got a pen?

16 The most common way of asking a question with the verb 'have' in the past is "Did you have a pen?"

17 Yes, I had my book with me last lesson.

18 Yes, it's easier to become good at a sport if you get lots of practice.

19 When we offer something to somebody, we can say "Would you like ...?"

20 Yes, I would like to visit Australia in the future. ~ No, I wouldn't like to visit Australia in the future.

Revision Exercise 23 (Lessons 50 – 51)

1   Give me an example of the word "therefore", please.

2   Can you hear the sound of traffic at the moment?

3   Is your house completely silent at night or can you hear street noise?

4   What's the difference between "a" and "an"?

5   Is it right to say "a hour" or "an hour"?

6   Did you fail to answer the last question?

7   What's the opposite of "to fail an exam"?

8   Did you have to get up early yesterday morning?

9 Which is it right to say: "You mustn't smoke in this building" or "You don't have to smoke in this building"?

10 Must you study ten hours a day if you want to learn English?

11 How do we sometimes form a noun from a verb?

12 Are you a complete beginner in English?

13 Who's your favourite writer?

14 Do you hope you'll live a very long time?

15 Do you believe everything people tell you?

16 What's the difference between "to do the shopping" and "to go shopping"?

17 Do you ever go shopping and come home with nothing?

18 Does good news put a smile on your face?

19 What are the three forms of an English verb?

20 What are the three forms of "give"?

Answers

1 I want to learn English well. Therefore, I must study.

2 Yes, I can hear the sound of traffic at the moment. ~ No, I can't hear the sound of traffic at the moment.

3 Yes, my house is completely silent at night. ~ No, my house isn't completely silent at night; I can hear street noise.

4 The difference between "a" and "an" is that we use "a" before a consonant sound whereas we use "an" before a vowel sound.

5 It's right to say "an hour".

6 No, I didn't fail to answer the last question; I succeeded in answering the last question.

7 The opposite of "to fail an exam" is "to pass an exam",

8 Yes, I had to get up early yesterday morning ~ No I didn't have to get up early yesterday morning.

9 It's right to say "You mustn't smoke in this building".

10 No, I don't have to study ten hours a day if I want to learn English.

11 We sometimes form a noun from a verb by adding the letters "er" to the verb.

12 No, I'm not a complete beginner in English; I began ...

13 My favourite writer is ...

14   Yes, I hope I'll live a very long time. ~ No, I don't hope I'll live a very long time.

15   No, I don't believe everything people tell me; some things I believe and some things I disbelieve.

16   The difference between "to do the shopping" and "to go shopping" is that "to do the shopping" means to buy the things that are necessary for the house, such as food etc., whereas "to go shopping" means to visit shops generally.

17   Yes, I sometimes go shopping and come home with nothing. ~ No, I never go shopping and come home with nothing; I always buy something.

18   Yes, good news puts a smile on my face.

19   The three forms of an English verb are the present, the past and the past participle.

20   The three forms of "give" are "give, gave, given".

Demonstration Charts

Chart 6

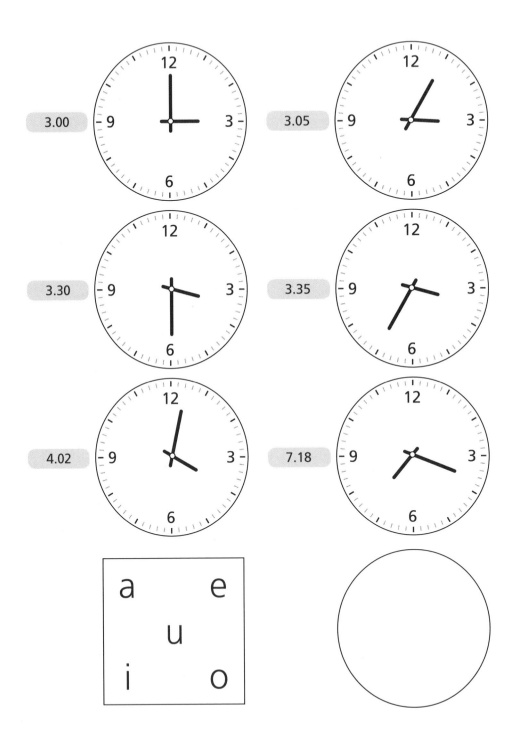

Chart 6

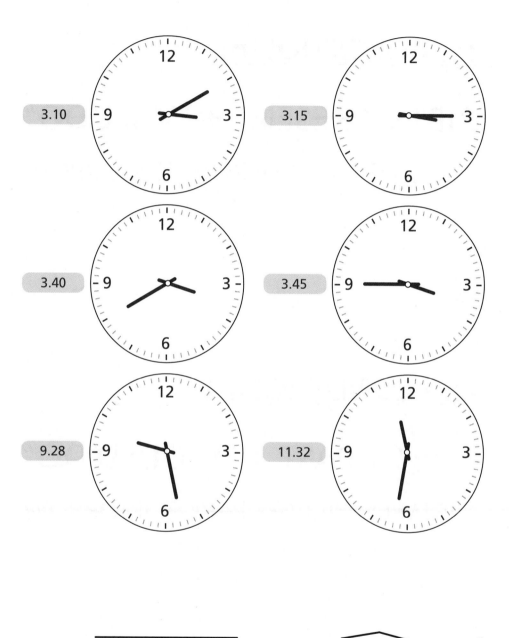

3.10

3.15

3.40

3.45

9.28

11.32

Chart 8

1st <u>CONDITIONAL</u>

"IF" + PRESENT + "WILL DO"

IF I GO TO THE PARK TOMORROW,

2nd <u>CONDITIONAL</u>

"IF" + PAST + "WOULD DO"

IF I WENT TO THE PARK TOMORROW,

Chart 8

= REAL POSSIBILITY

I WILL PLAY FOOTBALL

> This sentence means that I think there is a real possibility that I will go to the park tomorrow, and, if I do, I will play football.

= ONLY IMAGINING

I WOULD PLAY FOOTBALL

> This sentence means that I think it is very improbable that I will go to the park tomorrow; I am only imagining it.

INDEX

Index

STAGE 4
VOCABULARY

Arabic Vocabulary

Arabic vocabulary

Chinese Vocabulary

Chinese vocabulary

LESSON 54

LESSON 55

LESSON 56

LESSON 57

LESSON 58

LESSON 59

LESSON 60

Czech Vocabulary

Czech vocabulary

Czech vocabulary

LESSON 54

279 dream – dreamt – dreamt............. snít : přítomný čas - minulý čas - příčestí minulé
279 nightmare ....noční můra
279 garden ....zahrada
279 refuse ....odmítnout
279 separate ....samostatný/zvláštní/oddělený
280 lovely ....báječný/milý/pěkný
280 keep pokračovat/udržet/uchovat/ponechat/setrvat
280 continue...pokračovat
281 one ....jeden
281 you...ty
281 we...my
281 they..oni
281 mean ....znamenat/myslet/mínit
281 in general...obecně
281 necessarily ....nezbytně
281 in particular...konkrétně
281 ticket...vstupenka

LESSON 55

285 wild...divoký
285 branch ....větev/pobočka
285 bridge ....most
286 egg ....vejce
286 push..tlačit
286 pull...táhnout
286 interest ....zajímat
286 bore ....nudit
287 interesting...zajímavý
287 interested...zajímat se
287 boring ....nudný
287 bored ....znuděný
287 between..mezi (dvěma)
287 among ....mezi (více než dvěma)
287 science ....věda

LESSON 56

289 intention...záměr
289 soon... brzy
289 happen ....stát se
290 enjoy..užít si/mít rád
290 museum..muzeum
290 hole...otvor
290 keyhole..klíčová dírka
291 stupid...hloupý
291 intelligent ....inteligentní
291 clever...chytrý
291 against..proti
291 been ....příčestí minulé od "to be" (být)
291 gone ....příčestí minulé od "go" (jít)
291 return...vrátit se
293 bird ....pták
293 fly..letět
293 aeroplane (plane) ....letadlo

LESSON 57

294 fat ....tlustý
294 thin..hubený
294 swam............. minulý čas slovesa "swim" (plavat)
294 lostminulý čas a příčestí minulé od slovesa "lose" (ztratit)
295 each other ....navzájem (pro dva)
295 one another ....navzájem (pro více než dva)
296 to be able.................................moci/být schopen
297 factory...........................výrobní závod/továrna
297 ordinary ....běžný
297 paint...malovat
298 hotel..hotel

298 stay..ubytovat se

LESSON 58

299 song.. píseň
299 fun ....zábava/zábavný
299 funny...směšný/legrační
301 simply ....jednoduše
301 by mistake ....omylem
301 if..pokud
301 whether...zda
301 doubt ....pochybnost
303 speed...rychlost
303 surprise...........................překvapení/překvapit
303 struggle............................. zápas/úsilí/bojovat

LESSON 59

304 surround ....obklopovat
304 sword...meč
304 computer ....počítač
304 internet ....internet
304 website ....webové stránky
304 information..informace
304 turn on ....zapnout
304 turn off ....vypnout
305 great ....velký/skvělý/významný
305 lake...jezero
306 keptminulý čas a příčestí minulé od slovesa „keep" (držet)
306 promise...slib
306 keep a promise...................................dodržet slib
306 break a promise...................................porušit slib
306 found ..... minulý čas a příčestí minulé od slovesa „find" (najít)
307 else...jiný/další
307 fast...rychlý/rychle
308 music ....hudba
308 dance....................................tanec/tančit
308 rhythm ....rytmus
308 sense of rhythm.......................smysl pro rytmus
308 just..................................právě/jednoduše/pouze
308 done ....příčestí minulé od slovesa „do" (dělat/pomocné sloveso)
309 real ....skutečný

LESSON 60

310 probable ....pravděpodobný
310 improbable.........................nepravděpodobný
310 probably.................................pravděpodobně
310 possibility..možnost
310 imagine ....představit si
310 construction .... stavba
310 police...policie
310 police station ....policejní stanice
310 park ....park

French Vocabulary

French vocabulary

LESSON 47

242 queen ....reine
242 head ....tête / chef
242 blood..sang
242 offer ....offrir
242 company...compagnie
242 in company ....en compagnie
242 chocolate..chocolat
242 chocolates ....chocolats
242 life..vie
242 death ....mort
242 in the past.....................dans le passé / autrefois
243 suggest..suggérer
243 exercise...................................faire de l'exercice
244 tonight...ce soir
244 tired ....fatigué
244 tired of ....fatigué de
244 turn ....tourner
244 turn over ....retourner
245 got .... passé de "get"
...........................(trouver, acheter, aller, arriver)
245 until..jusqu'à (ce que)
245 till..jusqu'à
245 again........ une nouvelle fois / à nouveau / encore
245 too many..trop (de)
246 duration ....durée
246 there will be ....il y aura
246 there'll be...il y aura

LESSON 48

248 newspaper..journal
248 magazine.. magazine
248 popular ....populaire / réputé
248 sold.............................. passé de "sell" (vendre)
248 coal..charbon
248 decide..décider
248 menu ....menu
249 explain .... expliquer
249 heaven...paradis
249 hell..enfer
249 book..réserver
249 try .... essayer
249 try hard ....faire de son mieux / s'efforcer
249 possible ....possible
249 impossible ....impossible
250 quiet.......................tranquille / silencieux / calme
250 noisy...bruyant
250 sorry ....triste
250 pleased.. enchanté / ravi
250 I'm sorry.................................je suis désolé(e)
251 had ....passé de "have" (avoir)
251 could.........passé composé ou imparfait de "can"
....(pouvoir)
251 baby..bébé
252 perhaps ....peut-être
252 maybe...peut-être
252 a friend of yours....................un de tes /vos amis
252 sweet..sucré / bonbon

LESSON 49

254 spoken..parlé
254 written..écrit
255 spell ....épeler
255 communicate .... communiquer
255 easily..facilement
256 hadn't......... passé de "have" à la forme négative
257 practise............................pratiquer / s'entraîner
257 practice..........................pratique / entraînement

257 sport ....sport
258 would like.............. je/tu voudrais, il/elle voudrait,
.... nous voudrions, vous voudriez, iils/
....elles voudraient
258 visit .... visiter / se rendre à
258 Australia ....Australie
259 use / juːz/..utiliser
259 use /juːs/..utilisation

LESSON 50

260 therefore.......................... donc / par conséquent
260 sound..................son / bruit / sembler / avoir l'air
260 traffic......................................trafic / circulation
260 silent ....silencieux
262 succeed ....réussir
262 fail...échouer
262 examination (exam)................................examen
262 take an examination .... passer un examen
262 pass...réussir
262 have to..devoir

LESSON 51

264 worker............................. travailleur / travailleuse
264 beginner ....débutant / débutante
264 sleeper....................................dormeur / dormeuse
264 writer...écrivain
264 speaker.....................................orateur / oratrice
264 hope.....................................espérer / espoir
265 believe...croire
265 planet...planète
265 do the shopping.........................faire les courses
265 go shopping............................faire les magasins
265 list...liste
266 smile...sourire
266 tax.. taxe / impôt
267 past participle ....participe passé

LESSON 52

269 cat...chat
269 dog .... chien
269 result..résultat
269 lucky...chanceux
269 destroy..détruire
269 document...document
269 been ....été
269 Scotland ....Écosse
270 crime ....crime
270 guilty .... coupable
270 innocent...innocent
270 against the law ....contre la loi / illégal / illicite
270 I have eaten.................................j'ai mangé
270 experience.......................................expérience
271 for .... depuis / pendant
271 up to now..jusqu'à présent
272 too many..trop (de)
272 too much.. trop (de)
272 excessive..excessif

LESSON 53

274 age ....âge
274 marry ....se marier / épouser
274 get married ....se marier / épouser
274 average ....moyen
275 thick ....épais
275 thin..fin / mince
275 big...grand
275 little ....petit
275 Switzerland...Suisse
276 purse ....porte-monnaie
276 wallet .... portefeuille

German Vocabulary

German vocabulary

LESSON 41

211	wife - wives	Ehefrau - Ehefrauen
211	help	helfen
211	common	üblich
211	fire	Feuer
212	broad	breit
212	rich	reich
212	poor	arm
212	story	Geschichte
212	bedtime	Gute-Nacht-
212	express	ausdrücken
212	thought	Gedanke
213	irregular verbs	unregelmäßige Verben
213	so	also
213	change	verändern

LESSON 42

216	hill	Hügel
216	around	um
216	laugh	lachen
216	comedy	Komödie
216	enemy	Feind
216	Britain	Großbritannien
216	castle	Schloss
217	hungry	hungrig
217	noise	Geräusch
217	fact	Fakt
217	historical	historisch
217	mathematical	mathematisch
217	geographical	geografisch
217	become	werden
218	obtain	bekommen
218	fetch	holen
218	doctor	Arzt
218	get to	ankommen
218	reach	ankommen
219	there was	da war
219	there were	da waren
220	die	sterben
220	president	Präsident

LESSON 43

221	strong	stark
221	weak	schwach
221	physical	körperlich
221	soldier	Soldat
221	army	Armee
221	make money	Geld verdienen
221	uniform	Uniform
222	build	bauen
222	fill	füllen
222	contain	enthalten
222	art	Kunst
222	artist	Künstler / Künstlerin
222	feel	fühlen
222	too much	zu viel
223	middle	Mitte
223	centre	Mitte
224	sure	sicher
224	request	Bitte
224	neither ... nor	weder ... noch
225	willing	bereit

LESSON 44

226	film	Film
226	pronunciation	Aussprache
228	bicycle	Fahrrad
228	motorbike	Motorrad
228	bike	Fahrrad/Motorrad
228	mistake	Fehler
229	listen	zuhören
229	hear	hören
229	news	Nachrichten
229	radio	Radio
229	radio station	Radiosender
229	all the time	die ganze Zeit
229	ill	krank
229	well	gut
229	a cold	eine Erkältung
229	medicine	Medizin
230	favourite	Lieblings-
230	thirsty	durstig
230	programme	Sendung
230	sell	verkaufen
230	supermarket	Supermarkt

LESSON 45

232	lots of	viel
232	away	weg
232	tell	sagen
232	business	Geschäfte
232	foreign	ausländisch
233	rainy	verregnet
233	sunny	sonnig
233	cloudy	wolkig
233	nature	Natur
233	price	Preis
233	bush	Busch
234	worth	wert
234	to be worth	wert sein
234	value	Wert
235	hard	hart/schwer
235	soft	weich

LESSON 46

237	future tense	Futur
238	in 3 months' time	in 3 Monaten
239	won't	nicht werden
239	stay	bleiben
240	shall	sollen
240	suggestion	Vorschlag
240	public	Öffentlichkeit
240	in public	in der Öffentlichkeit
240	public holiday	Feiertag
241	show	zeigen
241	kill	töten

LESSON 47

241	tiger	Tiger
242	queen	Königin
242	head	Oberhaupt
242	blood	Blut
242	offer	anbieten
242	company	Gesellschaft
242	in company	in Gesellschaft
242	chocolate	Praline

German vocabulary

LESSON 54

279 dream - dreamt - dreamt ....träumen - träumte - geträumt
279 nightmare ....Alptraum
279 garden ....Garten
279 refuse ....sich weigern
279 separate ....separat
280 lovely .... schön / nett
280 keep......................weiterhin tun / aufbewahren / ....behalten / bleiben
280 continue...weiterhin tun
281 one ....man
281 you...man
281 we.. wir
281 they... sie
281 mean .... meinen
281 in general................................... im Allgemeinen
281 necessarily .... unbedingt
281 in particular.................................... insbesondere
281 ticket..Eintrittskarte

LESSON 55

285 wild ....wild
285 branch ....Ast/Zweigstelle
285 bridge ....Brücke
286 egg ....Ei
286 push...schieben
286 pull..ziehen
286 interest.. interessieren
286 bore ....langweilen
287 interesting...interessant
287 interested..interessiert
287 boring ....langweilig
287 bored ....gelangweilt
287 between.. zwischen
287 among ....unter/zwischen
287 science ....Wissenschaft

LESSON 56

289 intention.. Absicht
289 soon... bald
289 happen ....passieren / geschehen
290 enjoy...........................Spaß machen / genießen
290 museum... Museum
290 hole..Loch
290 keyhole ....Schlüsselloch
291 stupid...dumm
291 intelligent ....intelligent
291 clever..schlau
291 against...gegen
291 been ....war
291 gone ....gegangen
291 return..zurückkommen
293 bird ....Vogel
293 fly.. fliegen
293 aeroplane (plane) ....Flugzeug

LESSON 57

294 fat ....fett
294 thin..dünn
294 swam..schwamm
294 lost..verlor
295 each other ....einander
295 one another ....einander
296 to be able..können
297 factory..Fabrik
297 ordinary ....normal
297 paint..malen

298 hotel..Hotel
298 stay...übernachten

LESSON 58

299 song...Lied
299 fun .... Spaß
299 funny..lustig
301 simply .... einfach
301 by mistake ....aus Versehen
301 if.. wenn
301 whether... wenn/ob
301 doubt ....Zweifel
303 speed...Geschwindigkeit
303 surprise.................. Überraschung/überraschen
303 struggle........................ Kampf/Probleme haben

LESSON 59

304 surround ....umgeben
304 sword...Schwert
304 computer ....Computer
304 internet ....Internet
304 website ....Webseite
304 information....................................Informationen
304 turn on ....einschalten
304 turn off ....ausschalten
305 great ....toll/groß/wichtig
305 lake ....See
306 kept.. hielt
306 promise..Versprechen
306 keep a promise...............ein Versprechen halten
306 break a promise............ein Versprechen brechen
306 found ....fand
307 else .... sonst
307 fast..schnell
308 music...Musik
308 dance... tanzen
308 rhythm ....Rhythmus
308 sense of rhythm........................Rhythmusgefühl
308 just..gerade/nur/einfach
308 done .... gemacht
309 real .... echt

LESSON 60

310 probable .... wahrscheinlich
310 improbable........................... unwahrscheinlich
310 probably.................................... wahrscheinlich
310 possibility...Möglichkeit
310 imagine...vorstellen
310 construction ....Konstruktion
310 police .... Polizei
310 police station ....Polizeiwache
310 park ....Park

Italian Vocabulary

Italian vocabulary

Japanese Vocabulary

Japanese vocabulary

Polish Vocabulary

LESSON 54

LESSON 55

LESSON 56

LESSON 57

LESSON 58

LESSON 59

LESSON 60

Polish vocabulary

Portuguese Vocabulary

Portuguese vocabulary

Portuguese vocabulary

Portuguese vocabulary

Russian Vocabulary

LESSON 41

211 wife - wives................................. жена — жёны
211 help..помогать
211 common.............................. распространенный
211 fire ....камин
212 broad .... широкий
212 rich...богатый
212 poor .... бедный
212 story...рассказ
212 bedtime... перед сном
212 express .... выражать
212 thought ....мысль
213 irregular verbs ....неправильные глаголы
213 so... поэтому
213 change.. изменять

LESSON 42

216 hill...холм
216 around ....вблизи
216 laugh.. смеяться
216 comedy.. комедия
216 enemy... враг
216 Britain .... Британия
216 castle .... замок
217 hungry .... голодный
217 noise...шум
217 fact.. факт
217 historical .... исторический
217 mathematical........................ математический
217 geographical................................ географический
217 become..становиться
218 obtain .... получать
218 fetch................................ приносить, приводить
218 doctor .... доктор
218 get to .... приходить, добираться
218 reach...достигать
219 there was....................... там был (была, было)
219 there were .... там были
220 die... умирать
220 president.....................................президент

LESSON 43

221 strong .... сильный, крепкий
221 weak..слабый
221 physical ....физический
221 soldier...солдат
221 army .... армия
221 make money....................зарабатывать деньги
221 uniform .... униформа
222 build .... строить
222 fill...наполнять
222 contain..содержать
222 art .... искусство
222 artist...художник
222 feel..чувствовать себя
222 too much.............................слишком много
223 middle .... середина
223 centre .... центр
224 sure ....уверенный
224 request .... просьба
224 neither ... nor .... ни ... ни

225 willing......................готовый (сделать что-либо)
.............................охотно желающий что-либо

LESSON 44

226 film...фильм
226 pronunciation.............................произношение
228 bicycle .... велосипед
228 motorbike... мотоцикл
228 bike............................... велосипед/ мотоцикл
228 mistake................................ ошибка, ошибаться
229 listen .... слушать
229 hear .... слышать
229 news .... новости
229 radio .... радио
229 radio station..................................радиостанция
229 all the time............................... все время
229 ill .... больной
229 well ....здоровый
229 a cold... простуда
229 medicine...лекарство
230 favourite...любимый
230 thirsty................................ страдающий жаждой
230 programme .... программа
230 sell .... продавать
230 supermarket .... супермаркет

LESSON 45

232 lots of... много
232 away .... прочь go away = уходить,
....give ... away = отдавать,
..................................take ... away = уносить
232 tell... говорить
232 business ....бизнес
232 foreign ....иностранный
233 rainy...дождливый
233 sunny...солнечный
233 cloudy..облачно
233 nature...природа
233 price...стоимость
233 bush.. куст
234 worth..................стоящий; стоимость, ценность
234 to be worth..................................... стоить
234 value.................................стоимость, ценность
235 hard .... сложный, жесткий, усердно
235 soft .... мягкий

LESSON 46

237 future tense ....будущее время
238 in 3 months' time ....через 3 месяца
239 won't........ (отрицание в будущем времени)
239 stay...оставаться
240 shall......... (вспомогательный глагол будущего
времени)
240 suggestion .... предложение
240 public....................... общество, общественный
240 in public..публично
240 public holiday.........государственный праздник
241 show...показывать
241 kill ....убивать
241 tiger ....тигр

LESSON 47

242	queen	королева
242	head	глава
242	blood	кровь
242	offer	предлагать
242	company	компания
242	in company	в компании
242	chocolate	шоколад
242	chocolates	шоколадные конфеты
242	life	жизнь
242	death	смерть
242	in the past	в прошлом
243	suggest	предлагать
243	exercise	делать зарядку упражнение, тренировка; физическая нагрузка
244	tonight	сегодня вечером
244	tired	уставший
244	tired of	надоело, уставший от
244	turn	поворачивать
244	turn over	переворачивать
245	got	получил, пришел
245	until	до, (до тех пор) пока (не)
245	till	до
245	again	опять
245	too many	слишком много
246	duration	длительность
246	there will be	там будет
246	there'll be	там будет

LESSON 48

248	newspaper	газета
248	magazine	журнал
248	popular	популярный
248	sold	продал
248	coal	уголь
248	decide	решать
248	menu	меню
249	explain	объяснять
249	heaven	небеса, рай
249	hell	ад
249	book	резервировать
249	try	пробовать
249	try hard	упорно пытаться
249	possible	возможный
249	impossible	невозможный
250	quiet	тихий
250	noisy	шумный
250	sorry	сожалеющий
250	pleased	довольный
250	I'm sorry	я сожалею, извините
251	had	имел
251	could	мог
251	baby	малыш
252	perhaps	возможно
252	maybe	может быть
252	a friend of yours	твой/ваш друг
252	sweet	сладкий, сладость

LESSON 49

254	spoken	устный, разговорный
254	written	письменный
255	spell	писать/произносить по буквам
255	communicate	общаться
255	easily	легко
256	hadn't	не имел
257	practise	практиковать
257	practice	практика
257	sport	спорт

258	would like	хотел бы
258	visit	посещать
258	Australia	Австралия
259	use /juːz/	использовать
259	use /juːs/	применение, польза

LESSON 50

260	therefore	таким образом
260	sound	звук, шум, звучать
260	traffic	дорожное движение
260	silent	погруженный в тишину
262	succeed	добиваться успеха, преуспевать
262	fail	терпеть неудачу
262	examination (exam)	экзамен
262	take an examination	сдавать экзамен
262	pass	успешно сдавать (экзамен)
262	have to	должен

LESSON 51

264	worker	рабочий
264	beginner	начинающий
264	sleeper	соня
264	writer	писатель
264	speaker	оратор
264	hope	надеяться, надежда
265	believe	верить
265	planet	планета
265	do the shopping	делать покупки
265	go shopping	ходить по магазинам
265	list	список
266	smile	улыбаться, улыбка
266	tax	налог
267	past participle	причастие прошедшего времени

LESSON 52

269	cat	кот
269	dog	собака
269	result	результат
269	lucky	удачный, приносящий удачу, счастье
269	destroy	уничтожать, разрушать
269	document	документ
269	been	был, причастие прошедшего времени от be
269	Scotland	Шотландия
270	crime	преступление
270	guilty	виновный
270	innocent	невиновный
270	against the law	противозаконно
270	I have eaten	я съел
270	experience	опыт
271	for	на протяжении
271	up to now	до настоящего времени
272	too many	слишком много
272	too much	слишком много
272	excessive	излишний

LESSON 53

274	age	возраст
274	marry	жениться
274	get married	жениться
274	average	средний
275	thick	толстый
275	thin	тонкий
275	big	большой
275	little	маленький
275	Switzerland	Швейцария
276	purse	кошелек (женский)
276	wallet	бумажник

Slovak Vocabulary

LESSON 47

242 queen .... kráľovná
242 head .... hlava
242 blood.. krv
242 offer .... ponúknuť
242 company................................spoločnosť, firma
242 in company .... v spoločnosti, vo firme
242 chocolate...čokoláda
242 chocolates .... čokoládové cukríky
242 life...život
242 death .... smrť
242 in the past...........................v minulosti
243 suggest................................odporučiť, navrhnúť
243 exercise .... cvičenie
244 tonight.....................................dnes večer
244 tired .... unavený
244 tired of ....unavený z
244 turn .... otočiť (sa)
244 turn over ....obrátiť
245 got ....časť výrazu have got – mať
245 until.. až do
245 till... až do
245 again.................................... znova, opäť
245 too many.......................................priveľa
.... (s počítateľným podstatným menom)
246 duration .... trvanie
246 there will be ....bude
246 there'll be....................bude (skrátený tvar)

LESSON 48

248 newspaper....................................noviny
248 magazine....................................časopis
248 popular .... populárny, obľúbený
248 sold..... predaný (minulý čas slovesa predať (sell)
248 coal .... uhlie
248 decide................................rozhodnúť sa
248 menu .... menu
249 explain .... vysvetliť
249 heaven...nebo
249 hell..peklo
249 book.. rezervovať
249 try ....snažiť sa
249 try hard ....veľmi sa snažiť
249 possible .... možný
249 impossible .... nemožný
250 quiet..................................... tichý, pokojný
250 noisy...hlučný
250 sorry .... ľutovať
250 pleased .... potešený
250 I'm sorry.........................Je mi ľúto. Mrzí ma to.
251 had ....mal /minulý čas slovesa mať (have)
251 could.................................... mohol/-a by ...
251 baby... bábätko
252 perhaps .... snáď, možno
252 maybe...možno
252 a friend of yours................................ tvoj priateľ
252 sweet....................................... sladký, sladkosť

LESSON 49

254 spoken......................................hovorený
254 written.. písaný
255 spell...hláskovať
255 communicate................................komunikovať
255 easily ....ľahko
256 hadn't.......................................nemal /
........minulý čas slovesa mať v zápore (have not)
257 practise....................................precvičovať
257 practice...prax

LESSON 50

257 sport .... šport
258 would like.................................rád by
258 visit ....navštíviť
258 Australia ....Austrália
259 use /ju:z/.........................použiť, používať
259 use /ju:s/..použitie, účel

LESSON 50

260 therefore.......................................preto
260 sound...................................zvuk, znieť
260 traffic...............................doprava, premávka
260 silent...tichý
262 succeed .... uspieť
262 fail................................neuspieť, zlyhať
262 examination (exam)...................................skúška
262 take an examination ....robiť skúšku
262 pass...uspieť na skúške
262 have to.. musieť

LESSON 51

264 worker... pracovník
264 beginner .... začiatočník
264 sleeper... spáč
264 writer..spisovateľ
264 speaker......................................rečník
264 hope .... dúfať, nádej
265 believe ....veriť
265 planet..planéta
265 do the shopping...............................nakupovať
265 go shopping..................................ísť nakupovať
265 list ....zoznam
266 smile ....usmievať sa, úsmev
266 tax...daň
267 past participle ....príčastie minulé

LESSON 52

269 cat... mačka
269 dog .... pes
269 result..výsledok
269 lucky ....šťastný /majúci šťastie
269 destroy..zničiť
269 document...dokument
269 been ....minulé príčastie slovesa byť
269 Scotland ....Škótsko
270 crime ....zločin
270 guilty ....vinný
270 innocent...nevinný
270 against the law ....v rozpore so zákonom
270 I have eaten..Jedol som
270 experience.................................skúsenosť
271 for.. po dobu, počas
271 up to now.. až doteraz
272 too many.......priveľa (s počítateľným podstatným
menom)
272 too much..priveľa
.... (s nepočítateľným podstatným menom)
272 excessive......................................nadmerný

LESSON 53

274 age .... vek
274 marry ....ženiť sa/vydať sa
274 get married ....zosobášiť sa
274 average ....priemerný
275 thick...hrubý
275 thin...tenký
275 big..veľký
275 little.. malý
275 Switzerland.............................Švajčiarsko
276 purse .... peňaženka (dámska)
276 wallet .... peňaženka (pánska)

Spanish Vocabulary

Spanish vocabulary

LESSON 47

242 queen ....reina
242 head .... cabeza
242 blood...sangre
242 offer...ofrecer
242 company...compañía
242 in company ....en compañía
242 chocolate...chocolate
242 chocolates ....bombones
242 life... vida
242 death ....muerte
242 in the past..en el pasado
242 suggest...sugerir
243 exercise ....ejercicio
243 tonight.. esta noche
244 tired ....cansado/a/os/as
244 tired of ....cansado/a/os/as de
244 turn ....girar, dar vueltas; volverse
244 turn over ....pasar (páginas);
....darle la vuelta a algo
244 got ....pasado del verbo 'to get'
245 until...hasta
245 till..hasta
245 again................................... otra vez, de nuevo
245 too many....................................demasiados/as
245 duration ....duración
246 there will be ....habrá
246 there'll be..habrá
246 newspaper...periódico

LESSON 48

248 magazine.. revista
248 popular ....popular
248 sold................ pasado del verbo 'to sell' (vender)
248 coal...carbón
248 decide.. decidir
248 menu ....menú
248 explain...explicar
249 heaven..cielo
249 hell...infierno
249 book...reservar
249 try ....intentar, probar, tratar de
249 try hard ....hacer todo lo posible,
.... esforzarse mucho
249 possible ....posible
249 impossible ....imposible
249 quiet............tranquilo/a/os/as; silencioso/a/os/as
250 noisy...ruidoso/a/os/as
250 sorry ....triste/s, apenado/a/os/as
250 pleased.....................................contento/a/os/as
250 I'm sorry...lo siento
250 had ....pasado del verbo 'to have'
251 could...........................pasado de 'can' (poder)
251 baby...bebé
251 perhaps ....quizá, quizás, puede que
252 maybe......................quizá, quizás, puede que
252 a friend of yours...........................un amigo tuyo,
.... una amiga tuya
252 sweet.. dulce

LESSON 49

254 spoken.. hablado, oral
254 written......................................escrito, por escrito
254 spell...deletrear(se)
255 communicate......................................comunicar
255 easily..fácilmente
255 hadn't..........................contracción de 'had + not'
256 practise...practicar

257 practice...práctica
257 sport ....deporte
257 would like..gustaría
258 visit ....visitar
258 Australia ....Australia
258 use /juːz/..usar
259 use /juːs/..uso
259 therefore..por lo tanto

LESSON 50

260 sound.. sonar; sonido
260 traffic...tráfico
260 silent.....................en silencio; silencioso/a/os/as
260 succeed ....hacer algo con éxito
262 fail...................................suspender (un examen),
.... fracasar, fallar
262 examination (exam)................................ examen
262 take an examination .... hacer un examen
262 pass....................... aprobar (un examen), pasar
262 have to...tener que
262 worker.................................trabajador, trabajadora

LESSON 51

264 beginner ....principiante
264 sleeper................................persona que duerme
264 writer...escritor, escritora
264 speaker..................................... orador, oradora
264 hope ....esperar; esperanza
264 believe...creer
265 planet...planeta
265 do the shopping......................hacer los recados,
....hacer las compras
265 go shopping....................................ir de compras
265 list...lista
265 smile ....sonreir
266 tax...impuesto
266 past participle ....participio pasado

LESSON 52

269 cat...gato
269 dog...perro
269 result..resultado
269 lucky .... con suerte, afortunado/a/os/as
269 destroy..destruir
269 document...documento
269 been ....sido, estado
269 Scotland .... Escocia
269 crime...crimen
270 guilty...culpable
270 innocent.. inocente
270 against the law ....en contra de la ley
270 I have eaten.. he comido
270 experience...experiencia
270 for ....duración en el tiempo:
...............................'I've lived here for 3 years'
.... = he vivido aquí (durante,
.... desde hace) tres años
271 up to now........ hasta ahora, hasta este momento
271 too many...................................demasiados/as
272 too much.. demasiado
272 excessive................................. excesivo/a/os/as

LESSON 53

274 age ....edad
274 marry ....casar(se)
274 get married ....casarse
274 average .... media, promedio
274 thick .... grueso/a/os/as (para cosas)
275 thin.......delgado/a/os/as (para personas o cosas)
275 big..grande/s

Turkish Vocabulary

Turkish vocabulary

278 swimming pool.............................yüzme havuzu

LESSON 54

279 dream – dreamt – dreamt........rüya görmek/ rüya
279 nightmare .... kabus
279 garden .... bahçe
279 refuse ....reddetmek
279 separate ....ayrı
280 lovely ....Çok hoş
280 keep.. devam etmek/bulundurmak/tutmak/kalmak
280 continue.. devam etmek
281 one .... biri
281 you..sen
281 we.. biz
281 they...onlar
281 mean ....anlamına gelmek
281 in general.................................... genel olarak
281 necessarily ....ille de
281 in particular..özellikle
281 ticket.. bilet

LESSON 55

285 wild ....vahşi
285 branch .... dal/şube
285 bridge ....köprü
286 egg ....yumurta
286 push...itmek
286 pull...çekmek
286 interest...ilgisini çekmek
286 bore ....sıkmak
287 interesting..ilginç
287 interested..ilgili
287 boring ....sıkıcı
287 bored...sıkılmış
287 between...............................iki kişi/şey arasında
287 among .... ikiden fazla kişi/şey arasında
287 science ....fen

LESSON 56

289 intention.. niyet
289 soon............................birazdan/kısa süre içinde
289 happen .... olmak
290 enjoy ....zevk almak
290 museum... müze
290 hole..delik
290 keyhole... anahtar deliği
291 stupid.. aptal
291 intelligent ....zeki
291 clever...akıllı
291 against.................................... -e karşı/karşısında
291 been ...."to be - olmak" fiilinin 3. hali
291 gone ...."to go- gitmek" fiilinin 3. hali
291 return..geri dönmek
293 bird .... kuş
293 fly..uçmak
293 aeroplane (plane) ....uçak

LESSON 57

294 fat ....şişman
294 thin... zayıf
294 swam "to swim-yüzmek" filinin geçmiş zaman hali
294 lost "to lose- kaybetmek" fiilinin geçmiş zaman hali
295 each other ....birbirine
295 one another ....birbirlerine
296 to be able.. -ebilmek
297 factory...fabrika
297 ordinary ....normal
297 paint.. boyamak
298 hotel... otel
298 stay...kalmak

LESSON 58

299 song.. şarkı
299 fun .... eğlence
299 funny...komik
301 simply .... sadece
301 by mistake ....yanlışlıkla
301 if...eğer
301 whether....................eğer (şüpheli bir durumda)
301 doubt .... şüphe
303 speed.. hız
303 surprise...................................sürpriz/şaşırtmak
303 struggle...................................zorluk/zorlanmak

LESSON 59

304 surround ....çevrelemek
304 sword...kılıç
304 computer ....bilgisayar
304 internet ....internet
304 website ....internet sitesi
304 information...bilgi
304 turn on .... açmak
304 turn off .... kapatmak
305 great ....büyük/çok iyi/önemli
305 lake... göl
306 kept................"to keep=tutmak" filinin geçmiş hali
306 promise...söz vermek
306 keep a promise...........................sözünü tutmak
306 break a promise......................sözünü tutmamak
306 found .... "to find-bulmak" fiilinin geçmiş hali
307 else... daha başka
307 fast.. hızlı
308 music ....müzik
308 dance .... dans etmek
308 rhythm ....ritim
308 sense of rhythm............................ritim duygusu
308 just.................................... az önce/sadece/yalnız
308 done .... "to do - yapmak" fiilinin 3. hali
309 real ....gerçek

LESSON 60

310 probable .... muhtemel
310 improbable............ olanaksız/muhtemel olmayan
310 probably.................................büyük bir ihtimalle
310 possibility...olasılık
310 imagine...hayal etmek
310 construction.. yapı
310 police..polis
310 police station ....polis karakolu
310 park ....park

Turkish vocabulary

Notes